In My Lifetime

In My Lifetime

William S. Hart

Copyright © 2011 by William S. Hart.

Library of Congress Control Number: 2011903194
ISBN: Hardcover   978-1-4568-7763-7
               Softcover   978-1-4568-7762-0
               Ebook   978-1-4568-7764-4

This book was printed in the United States of America.

Compiled and Edited by Christie Levandowski

Bill Hart's memories of the 1920s, '30s and '40s became a monthly column in the Granby *Drummer*. From milking cows and gathering eggs on the North Granby farm to wartime training as a bomber navigator, Hart shared a lifetime of memories. Some articles are just as they appeared in the *Drummer, Southwoods* Magazine or in other publications. Some, such as those about the Godard farm, which Bill described in many of his columns, have been compiled and edited to eliminate duplication.

To order additional copies of this book, contact:
Xlibris Corporation
1-888-795-4274
www.Xlibris.com
Orders@Xlibris.com
91497

Contents

Acknowledgements

My thanks to **Citizens for a Better Granby** and the Granby *Drummer* for underwriting this project in celebration of Granby's 225th Anniversary. Since 1970, Citizens For a Better Granby has published The Granby *Drummer*, a monthly, all-volunteer community newspaper.

And a special thanks to those who contributed to the images that make this book so special, and to:

Peter Dinella, who is an award-winning Granby photographer, and contributed original photos and much appreciated expertise to this project;

the **Salmon Brook Historical Society** for sharing its photo archives; and finally, thanks to **Dave Tolli** and **Andrea Leshinskie** for volunteering their digital image expertise in preparing many of the vintage photos.

The old Godard farmhouse in the late 1800s. L to R: George Seymour Godard,
Harvy Godard and Oliver "Ollie" Godard. W. S. Hart photo

THE GODARD FARM

Days on a rural farm started at dawn and ended at dark during the 1920s and the depression years of the 1930s. Every member of the family put in long hours of manual labor keeping those farms going through difficult times.

On the Hart side of my family, I've traced my grandparents to their arrival from Germany in 1850 but can trace them no farther back. On my mother's side, the Godards of North Granby, I have ties to the first settlers of Granby when it was still part of ancient Simsbury. In my search, I stumbled upon a 1677 deed showing the family owned thirty acres of land on the northwest corner of the Barn Door Hills.

My mother, Grace Minerva Godard, was born in 1890 in the house now owned by Dr. Harry and Susan Werner on Godard Road in North Granby. In the late 1920s we lived there for a short time with my grandfather, Oren Godard. In the '30s, during my teen years, I spent summers working the family farm with my Uncle Beach Godard. I also went there for winter and spring vacations and every other opportunity I got.

The place was at the end of a long, narrow dirt road with fields on one side and a tobacco barn and a horse barn on the other. In the beginning there wasn't any central heating so the warmth came from fireplaces and an iron woodstove in the kitchen. There was no electricity. In the evening, the family read, played games and did handwork by the light from a kerosene lamp in the center of the dining table. There was a party-line telephone.

The fourteen-room farmhouse on the hill looked over open fields to the millpond at the corner of Granville Road and Silver Street where a two-hundred-year-old gristmill stood above the gorge. From the porch we saw the top of Great Craig Mountain and watched red tailed hawks soaring on high looking for small game. Turkey vultures were frequent visitors, silently gliding in circles on unmoving wings searching for carrion. Today, the fields have grown to heavy forest and the millpond is all but silted in.

In the 1920s, Granville Road and Great Uncle Ollie's farm just north of the pond were clearly visible. Sound carried across the open fields so well that when a visitor pulled into his driveway, snatches of their conversation were heard on our front porch.

Ollie Godard's house and barns viewed from Godard Road.
The house stands just north of Silver Street and the millpond.
Portions of the barn foundations still stand. SBHS photo

Between 1880 and 1920 the farm was a success because income came from several sources. The mainstay was a dairy herd of thirty milking cows. The up-and-down saw mill, a grist mill, orchards, chickens, tobacco, raising and training horses, supplying teams for hire, selling ties to the railroad and a small stagecoach franchise were all profitable sidelines.

My mother was the only girl of seven children. My grandmother had the help of a hired girl from the local orphanage. The farm operations required two or three hired men. I have a diary in which grandmother wrote: "we sat eighteen for supper last night."

My grandparents, Oren and Lena Godard. W. S. Hart photo

My mother, Grace Hart Peek. W. S. Hart photo

Grandmother prepared and cooked three meals a day for all of them and still made time to can garden vegetables and fruit for the winter, make clothes for the children and clean and keep the house in order. Almost daily entries in her 1881 diary repeated this similar description: "made 7 loaves of bread, 6 pies, a card of gingerbread, a pan of cookies, baked a pan of beans."

In those years, the Granby Depot was an active place with steam trains whistling in and out at all hours. My Grandmother Lena's diaries from the 1850s mention having fresh oysters and bluefish. Reading further I found that her brother, George White, worked at the Fulton Fish Market in New York City. He'd pack the fish in ice, put it on the train, and later that day Grandpa Oren hitched up the horse and buggy and picked it up at Granby Depot. That's faster than we can do it today.

The Depression years

By the time I got there in 1932, at age ten, the farm had been reduced to the dairy and a small egg business struggling to survive the Depression. Most farms were in poverty. The houses weren't painted. The lawn, if they had one, grew wild. The roads were a quagmire in spring, a dust cloud in summer and unplowed in winter.

My uncle's farm still had no running water other than from a hand pump in the kitchen. There was no electricity or inside plumbing. However, several fireplaces had been blocked off and a wood-fired hot air furnace sent hot air through floor registers in the living and dining rooms. The only other heat was from the iron stove in the kitchen.

In those depression years farmers had little ready cash so a large vegetable garden was a necessity. Next to the chicken house we plowed a one-quarter-acre vegetable garden that was weeded, suckered and sprayed for ants. The ongoing harvest of peas, beans, carrots, potatoes, sweet corn, kale, radishes, cucumbers and tomatoes was picked, cleaned and came to the table fresh or was canned—put by—for the winter ahead.

The women tended the garden, took care of the chickens and did the washing and ironing without electricity. The sewing was done on a machine powered with a foot treadle. Of course, the woman also tended to the children, prepared and cooked meals, baked and did volumes of dishes and pots and pans with coarse soap and water heated on the wood stove.

One hundred laying hens guaranteed we didn't have idle time on our hands. Each day they were watered and fed and their manure removed.

The profit came from collecting the eggs, grading them, and taking them to market. Some of those eggs found their way to Aunt Marie's kitchen for baking, breakfast and other meals.

Once in a while we had fresh game and brook trout. When a cow aged and no longer maintained a profitable milk output, it was slaughtered. Toughened by the daily trip up and down the mountain we used for pasture, that meat was chewy.

In 1935, Check Bread and Bond Bread started driving small panel delivery trucks out into the countryside to serve the far-flung farms. The concept caught on and other outfits such as Stanley Home Products and Raleigh Products soon found their way to our door.

A Mr. Bronson, who lived on Old Messenger Road in West Granby, became innovative and outfitted his old Model T Ford truck with a wood-paneled body that he painted dark brown. He loaded it with all kinds of meats and went farm to farm. Late on summer Saturday afternoons, we heard the sound of that truck's struggling old engine chugging up the dirt road with the dust sucking in behind it. Mr. Bronson stopped in the yard and stepped down wearing a straw boater hat and a white apron spotted with the stains of his trade. He went to the rear and dropped the short tailgate with an attached cutting board. The upper door, above the tailgate, lifted up on hinges and was propped up by two thin rods at opposite sides. If it was stormy, Mr. Bronson and Aunt Marie stood under the shelter.

Mr. Bronson hung a circular brass-faced scale with black numbers and black pointer and, from a small hook at its base, he suspended a white metal tray with a hanger shaped in the outline of a beehive or dome.

Aunt Marie folded her arms over her ample bosom and asked the prices of such things as pot roast, chuck, liver, tongue, pork, bacon, hot dogs or sausage.

She never asked about chicken. We had our own supply.

Unfortunately we only killed a chicken after it stopped laying eggs. By then it was old and tough and could only be eaten fricasseed. The skin was a quarter-inch thick and difficult to chew, but the white gravy and dumplings were great.

When I see beautiful plump chickens neatly wrapped in cellophane on display in the

Marie Godard, wife of Beach Godard. W. S. Hart photo

supermarket, they bring to mind a very different scene. In yesteryear the old hen's neck was put on the chopping block and the axe quickly ended it all. The legs were removed at the knee and the entrails removed. Then it was placed in a big kettle of boiling water that had just come off the wood stove. After a few minutes of soaking, the feathers were pulled out by hand. The remaining pinfeathers were singed off over a candle flame, and after a thorough washing, the bird was quartered and cooked.

I wasn't always so good with chickens. When I was five years old I was in the barnyard eating a box of Cracker Jacks when I disturbed a mother hen and her brood. She came squawking at me with her wings outspread and claws flailing. I was so scared, I ran sobbing to my mother as fast as my pudgy little legs would go, my arms pumping and the box swinging in wide arcs scattering popcorn and peanuts.

Later, when I was in my teens, my city friends visited me on the farm. I'd show them the chickens and throw out some feed and "scratch," and we'd listen to the clucking as the hens pecked away. I told the guys I could stand in one spot and drive all the chickens into the hen house. Chickens have an inborn fear of hawks, particularly the red tailed hawk with its high whistling call. I stood still and gave an intermittent high-pitched whistle. The hens stopped pecking and cocked their heads from side to side. Very slowly they turned and gingerly stepping along, sought the safety of the hen house.

The "necessary" and the bathtub

With no indoor plumbing we used a privy. Beyond the kitchen, through the cluttered mudroom and across the dirt-floored woodshed, one reached the privy that was attached to the end of the shed. On a cold winter's night a trip to the "necessary" was an experience. One lit a small hand-held lamp and headed out. The shadows cast moving images on the rafters of the woodshed. Had a skunk or some other animal come in through the open side to seek shelter? One moved quickly to the privy. There was no insulation and, by the nature of the structure, there were openings that exposed you to the swirling winds. You did not tarry long.

Winter baths were a chore. Pails filled with water at the kitchen pump were heated on the woodstove. The hot water was emptied into a circular galvanized tub about three feet in diameter and a foot deep that was placed in front of the open fireplace. After rinsing off, I remember standing up and steam rising from my body. The coarse towel had no resemblance to the soft Turkish ones we have today.

Quickly pulling on a flannel nightshirt and a pair of wool stockings, I ran up the steep back stairs clutching a small lamp in one hand and the flat hand railing with the other. I passed through the shadowy hallway to my front room and dove into a double bed with a horsehair mattress and down-filled pillows.

The mattress on that double, wooden-slatted bed was not a Posturepedic. It was stuffed with horsehair and it was impossible to sleep crosswise because through the years a ridge had formed down the middle of the mattress. It sagged, forcing me to sleep on my back or partly on my side. A one-handled china pot under the bed made chilly nocturnal visits to the windy outhouse unnecessary.

Only my nose stuck out from under the blankets and comforter. There was no heat upstairs and on a night with temperatures in the teens, the upstairs rooms were well below freezing. Some nights a scratchy piece of horsehair worked its way through the ticking and my nightshirt to add a little extra discomfort.

In that bed, on warm spring nights, I listened to the first peepers in the swamp. Spring freshets and the snowmelt coming down from the mountains created a muted roar as the water ran over the dam and through the gorge. In summer the roar became the quiet, relaxing sound of calm water flowing over the rocks. The bullfrogs in the pond by the horse barn broke the silence with spasmodic croaking that sounded like "knee-deep, knee-deep." About the second week in August the katydids joined in. These nighttime noises, and the wind rustling through the leaves of the shagbark hickory tree, created a primitive symphony.

In the middle thirties, with help from the family, the house was electrified, running water was piped from a mountain spring and, at last, there was inside plumbing. The farm became part of the modern world with a Philco radio that brought news of farm prices and entertained us with programs like One Man's Family and Jack Armstrong The All American Boy.

Even with those improvements, during the Depression years there was no money or credit to buy tractors or other farm equipment. Occasionally my aunt got part-time employment doing piecework at the Cooley Drum Shop in Granville, Massachusetts. Other times she sorted apples at Peck's Orchard in North Granby. Cash was hard to come by. Near the end of the month I'd often pedal my Elgin bicycle from Sears and Roebuck down the dirt road to the mailbox by the gorge. Hopefully, Great Uncle Porter, a successful judge in Kansas City, had sent a fifty-dollar check so we might go on another month. If it came, we had a treat. The one I remember best was vanilla, chocolate and strawberry flavored Neapolitan ice cream.

The Belgian team

I purchased this statue of Belgian draft horses because it so closely resembles Prince and Colonel. Peter Dinella photo

Without a tractor, all of the heavy work was done with a team of workhorses. Uncle Ollie's team of Belgian draft horses was a living, breathing part of our farm existence. Prince and Colonel were well cared for and that meant periodically replacing their shoes. My uncle had a small hand-blown forge to heat the horseshoes red hot so he could shape them to fit the hooves.

He'd put his back to the horse, lift its leg and hold it between his knees. After removing the old shoe, he used a coarse file to smooth the hoof and the shavings on the floor looked like shredded coconut. A new, heated shoe was modified with a hammer on the anvil for a good fit and nailed to the horse's hoof; a painless operation that kept the horses' feet healthy and comfortable for work.

Those wonderful Belgians were brushed and combed daily and the huge animals appreciated the attention. Each turned its head to look at you if you called him by name.

Sitting on the porch with the grown-ups could get pretty boring for a kid. Some evenings I pulled out the old sidesaddle my mother had used as a girl and cinched it up on one of the big Belgians. I'd sit on my high perch, making a quiet "tch-tch" sound with my tongue, while the animal slowly clopped around the farm paths with an occasional snort.

My favorite horse was Prince. Even now, sixty-five years later, I can feel his soft, velvety nose and see the long, sparse silvery hairs in his wide nostrils. Prince's huge lidded eyes seemed so intelligent. I even enjoyed currycombing those broad sides and backs and brushing out their manes and tails.

When the horses died in the mid 30s, we found a junk car, removed the body and put a truck rear-end in it. It became the workhorse—pulling the horse-drawn equipment that hauled and spread manure, plowed and cultivated, cut hay and harvested the corn and drew it to the tall silo.

I was then fourteen, and to help my uncle I had to learn to drive that vehicle. One day we jumped into the family car, a 1928 Whippet with wooden-spoke wheels, and drove to the empty corn lot. He told me about the starter, gearshift, clutch, and starter and said, "go to it" and walked away. I stalled the old car, ground the gears, flooded the engine and almost tipped it over but I did learn how to drive.

Haying and harvesting the corn crop

Uncle Beach cut the hay with a John Deere mowing machine, a team of workhorses and later, the improvised tractor. When dry, the hay was formed into windrows with a one-horse hay rake that had two high metal wheels and a long curved row of downward-pointing tines.

I used a pitchfork to roll the windrows into haycocks and finally loaded it on the hay wagon that had a homemade wooden rack. Uncle Beach forked the haycocks onto the wagon and I stowed them so they could be unloaded and tossed into the barn's haymow without falling apart. Sometimes we were caught by a quick thunderstorm and had to spread the windrows or haycocks out to dry again either by hand or with a one-horse tedder. A tedder is a two-wheeled device with circular, revolving forks that lift and turn the hay to dry it quickly or after a rain shower.

In late August we cut the fields again for the rowens (a New England term for the second cutting) to hold us through the winter. When that was done it was time to harvest the corn.

John Deere equipment also harvested field corn for the cows. The harvester was pulled down a row and two flat blades set in a V-shape cut the standing corn about six inches from the ground. The cut stalks were gathered into a standing position inside the machine. When there were enough stalks to make a bundle, maybe thirty or so, a piece of heavy twine automatically pulled it together and tied a knot about three feet up. The bundle was kicked out the side of the harvester and fell on the ground at a right angle to the cut cornrow.

After enough corn was down, a wagon was drawn along the rows at a walking pace. Walking behind the wagon, each bundle was grabbed by the twine with your left hand while your right seized the bases of the stalks. Each bundle was thrown onto the wagon with the butt ends facing the rear.

At the silo, the wagon was drawn up to the conveyor table of the John Deere corn blower with the butts ready to be tossed onto the moving belt. The bundles were pushed into rotating cutting blades that diced the corn stalks up and blew the resulting silage up an eight-inch-diameter galvanized pipe that emptied into the top of the silo.

The rigid pipe only blew in one direction so silage mounded on the far side of the silo. Periodically we used a five-tined fork to spread it around evenly and then stomped it down. As the level silage rose, two-foot-square wooden doors, each fitted with an iron step, were stacked into the open slot that went vertically up the silo. This side was accessible from inside the barn so silage could be removed to feed the cows. Eventually these doors reached the top of the silo and were removed during the winter as the ensilage was used. The stored hay and ensilage fed the stock when outside grazing fields were snow covered and frozen and were supplemented with grain bought from the feed store in burlap bags.

Cows, calves and the cow barn

Twice a day up to twenty-five cows had to be milked by hand, fed and groomed and the manure in the trough behind the cows shoveled out the barn door to a two-wheeled wagon. When full, it was drawn to the cornfields and the manure spread with a John Deere manure spreader.

The barn was perfectly comfortable in winter because the cows' body heat and the low ceiling kept it at a fairly constant temperature. In summer it became unbearable.

In those ancient summers I most vividly recall the ongoing battle with the swarms of flies. We hung coils of flypaper and used a fly swatter made of a small piece of window screen with a cloth edge. A later version made of thin rubber and in the same shape didn't work as well. As the cows came in from pasture, I stood by the door with a hand-pumped spray gun filled with Flit. It killed the flies I managed to hit but the barn was still filled with them.

At milking time, I sat down on a small wooden stool and held a clean, shiny pail between my knees. I pinched the end of the cow's tail behind my left knee so it couldn't swat me. The cows' deep breathing along with the spasmodic scraping of huge tongues licking grain from the cement floor in front of the stanchion were familiar barn sounds. With the first squirts of warm milk, as the cow "let down," there was a pinging sound of two sharp streams hitting the bottom of the empty pail. As the pail filled, the sound became deeper, and near the end when the pail was about full, it turned softer as the squirts pierced the thick foam.

Two barn cats always sat in the aisle waiting for me to squirt a stream of warm milk at them. They tried to catch the milk in their mouths but mostly licked it from their paws after wiping it off their fur.

When outside temperatures reached the eighties and nineties, the cows and the low ceiling created a steam bath. Pores opened up with sweat, soaking your clothes and your hair. It dripped from eyebrows and nose and ran down your chest and back. Wet hands slipped off the teats on the down pull. If the herd was dripping wet from a heavy thunderstorm, the problem was compounded. And all the while, the flies swarmed around your face and neck.

In 1936, when a local farmer went out of business, we bought his used milking machine. It was run by a compressor that we powered with a "one-lunger" or make-and-break water-cooled engine. It made life easier.

No matter the time of year, the milk had to be picked up and transported to the Miller Dairy in Bloomfield for processing and bottling. With the exception of the College Highway (Route 10), the majority of Granby roads were dirt. That was all right most of the time, but in springtime those roads became a muddy quagmire. In winter, they were rutted with frozen puddles and covered with drifted snow.

The road leading up to the farm from Granville Road was kept open in winter by a V-type snow plow made from a couple of planks that Uncle Beach pulled with the team of Belgians. The milk truck aided his plowing. Its dual rear wheels broke through the deep drifts to get to the milk house. Some storms dropped more snow than our plow or the milk truck could deal with. The 1928 Whippet, and later the 1932 Essex, sat in the barn until the snow melted enough to clear or the plow got to us. During spring mud season the cars sat many a day waiting for the roads to be passable.

Milk production depends upon the cow producing a calf each year and the calf being quickly weaned. When our records showed a cow was about due, we confined her to her stanchion in the barn. Occasionally we misjudged and that caused some problems. The resulting birthing sometimes had comical results.

The pasture started at the rear of the barn and immediately went up the steep mountainside slope. Three quarters of it was cleared for grazing but the remainder was overgrown with dense clumps of juniper and brush. We knew we'd missed the cow's due date when she failed to come down the mountain at milking time with the rest of the herd; that meant we had to go searching.

By instinct, going back to the beginning of time, a cow seeks out a secluded area in the brush and tramps around in increasing larger circles to flatten the brush to use as a bed. After the calf is born the mother licks it clean, happy in her seclusion with her new offspring greedily sucking away.

When we found the spot our new mother had chosen, her newborn bleated loudly in fear. Its young, unsteady legs were not strong enough to follow the mother down the steep slope so one of us draped the calf around his neck and trudged back to the barn.

The new arrival was content to be under cover with nothing to do but get nourishment. That was all right for a few days, but it had to be weaned away from its mother. We used a glass bottle full of warm milk. We pulled the calf from the teat and substituted a thumb, which was greedily accepted. This only lasted for an instant before the bottle was substituted for the thumb. After a few days, we put some grain and milk into a pail. It was no chore to put the calf's head and the bottle into the pail and then remove the bottle; the greedy calf easily learned to lap up the formula. Shortly after that, we graduated the calf to a mix of hay, grain and ensilage.

I was always up with the sun. One morning I awoke and immediately thought of the big black and white Holstein we'd kept in her stanchion all night because she was due to have a calf.

It was around 5 a.m. when I went out to get the barn ready to bring the herd in from the pasture for milking. I noticed the mother-to-be was standing in the stanchion, and saw small hooves just starting to emerge. I ran back to the house and woke my uncle. He rolled over and said he'd be out shortly.

Well, I thought a cow should lie down to give birth but this one was standing, which meant the calf would fall onto the cement floor. I grabbed an empty burlap grain bag, put it across my arms and stood behind the cow to catch the calf as it emerged. I set the new born calf down and shortly the cow licked it clean.

Over the next few days I weaned the calf to a Coke bottle filled with warm milk and then to a pail of milk and grain. Throughout the summer I watched the calf grow with a sense of pride that I had helped bring it safely into the world.

Sam Goldschmidt and his family ran the North Granby general store and the Post Office. He also dealt in livestock and chickens, and he came to the farm to buy calves. These transactions were interesting to observe. Both Sam and Uncle Beach knew the market value of calves because they listened to Frank Atwood on WTIC radio. Atwood started his early morning weekday broadcasts with farm news and the latest market prices for farm commodities.

If the going price for a calf were seven dollars, Sam told Uncle Beach the market was off. If we had a bull calf, he'd say heifers were drawing the good price. Goldschmidt always commented that he'd always liked Beach and had done business with him for a long time, so he'd help him out by giving him four dollars for the calf.

Uncle Beach countered that the calf came from one of his best milkers and he planned to raise it himself, but for ten dollars he'd let it go. They'd hem and haw back and forth talking about veal and feed prices and the value of hides, and at last they'd agree on seven dollars—the market price. The calf was loaded on the truck, and as Sam left, I could almost hear each one privately chuckling over how he'd outdone the other.

After the chores were done

On occasion, after the evening milking chores were done and supper finished, Uncle Beach, Aunt Marie, my two girl cousins and I piled into the four-door 1928 Whippet. We'd drive some five or six miles to Vining Hill Road in Southwick, Massachusetts to visit either Frank Steere and his wife or my aunt's parents, the Frank Holcombs.

In those days, with no rural electricity, their homes were lit with kerosene lamps that cast odd shadows on the ceilings and walls. Usually the women congregated in the living room and talked of the things women had in common while the men went to the kitchen by the wood stove, smoked and swapped stories.

There was man talk of farm problems, milk prices and the high cost of grain and seed. On the lighter side I learned about hunting coon, fox, pheasant and ducks. Trapping was mentioned and, of course, stream and ice fishing were favored topics.

I learned about treating spavin, which is peculiar to the hock on a horse, and how to cure a bruised fetlock. With what I learned from those men I was able to help that cow with a difficult calving.

Listening to the tales they shared, I came to realize that in their youth these men did worse pranks on Halloween than anything we kids had yet dreamed up. It took a bit of doing to dismantle a buggy and reassemble it on the roof of a town building. And I still marvel at the story of leading a horse up three flights of stairs, and leaving it to be discovered when the business opened the next morning.

Applejack

Prohibition was on, and my father cautioned me not to tell my schoolmates what was going on at the farm on Sunday afternoons in winter. The barn across from the house was used to strip tobacco leaves from the plants grown on the farm. The hard dirt floor was a two-foot step down and deep, waist-high counters lined the walls under rows of windows that provided light to strip leaves.

My father, uncle and their cronies set a three-burner kerosene stove in the middle of the room. The stove's blue enamel cylinders had Isinglass portals through which the orange glow of the flames was visible.

Their homemade still consisted of an oblong copper wash kettle that sat on top of the stove with a long copper tube soldered to the cover. The tube went over the side of the stove and formed a descending coil inside a fifty-gallon cider barrel. The coil emptied into a bucket on the floor.

Hard cider fermented from apples grown in our orchard was boiled in the kettle. The barrel was filled with snow, and when the steam from the boiling cider went through the snow-packed coils it condensed. The resulting liquid collected in the bucket. That potent liquid went through the still three times. The resulting cider brandy or applejack was, according to them, 120-proof or 60% alcohol. Those clandestine Sunday afternoons ended when Prohibition was repealed.

Autumn mornings

By autumn, the days were getting shorter and the evenings were not so warm as they had been. But it's autumn mornings that I recall best.

On early fall mornings, I wanted to stay in my comfortable snug bed. The dark morning air was chilly and the sun seemed to rise so slowly from way beyond the foliated hills.

The clear icy-cold water from the black kitchen pump that I splashed on my face woke me up in a hurry. After getting the kindling going and shaking down the ash, the snapping wood fire in the old iron stove began to warm the kitchen.

Walking from the house to the barns my shoes got wet with the heavy dew clinging to the blades of grass: even the cobwebs on the greenery were sprinkled with moisture.

The docile black and white Holstein cows waited by the wooden gate patiently chewing their cuds.

Often the team of horses was down by the small stream peacefully munching on clumps of grass. I could see and hear their breath in the quiet autumn air.

Through the haze that was just starting to clear, I made out the hillside orchard with ripe Macintosh apples showing fiery red in contrast to the green juniper bushes nearby.

Down the narrow dirt road, beside the fields where the corn had already been cut, I could see Queen Ann's lace and plentiful yellow goldenrod.

Later, after we finished the milking chores, we turned the cows out again, and they slowly trudged out to the mountainside pasture.

We walked back to the old kitchen for a big breakfast of ham and eggs and my aunt's warm homemade bread, and washed it down with a mug of hot coffee laced with our own cream.

The busy days of buttoning up the farm for winter went on their relentless way, and a feeling of contentment seemed to settle over all of us. But it's still the mornings I fondly recall.

Winter chores

One of the biggest chores was supplying wood for the house, and in winter we spent three days every two weeks filling the woodshed. We maintained a wood lot—out past the cornfield and the watermelon lot—to fuel the wood stove, the hot air furnace and the fireplaces.

There were no power saws so trees were felled with a Collins axe and limbed out. One day was spent doing this and the next day we hitched a team of horses to a bobsled or bobsleigh—two double-runner sleds held together by a pole called a "reach." In the woodlot, the small trees were chained onto the sleigh and hauled to the woodshed.

There the trees were cut to length with a circular saw powered by a wide pulley belt attached to the rear wheel of a 1918 Maxwell automobile long since taken from the road. I stood beside the saw blade as Uncle Beach fed the tree into the saw. I grabbed the pieces and threw them into the shed behind me. Finally the wood, in lengths appropriate for the wood stove, fireplace or furnace, were split with an axe on the chopping block and stacked in the woodshed.

Ice was a necessity for keeping perishable food and milk in warm weather, and on hot summer days, the luxury of a cold drink. Before electricity came to the farm, harvesting and storing ice was another wintertime chore.

Several men, using long saws with a handle at one end, cut parallel lines through the thick ice, measured it, cut it into blocks and, with iron tongs, hauled it from the water onto a sled. The team drew the sled to the icehouse where the ice was stored for spring and summer use.

Our icehouse was fifteen-foot square with a tall door in one of its four double walls. The foot-wide space between the walls was filled with sawdust. Sawdust was also packed around the ice blocks as insulation to prevent the blocks from melting or freezing together.

Fire was one of the hazards of an icehouse. Apparently the sawdust fermented, producing wood alcohol that could ignite from spontaneous combustion and burn the building to the ground.

Thoughts of a time gone by

All my old relatives are gone, the farm long since sold, and the open land grown back to forest. In my memory I still see the old pasture, mowing land, cornfields, horse and cow barns and the blue silo.

I hear the animal sounds, the hen clucking over her brood and the small stream gurgling over the mossy rocks.

I smell the earth, the drying hay, the cut corn, the wood smoke, the manure and the human sweat.

Again I wash up at the pump, and sit at a table laden with the food we'd grown and listen to the small talk of crops, church affairs, relatives and fellow farmers and their problems.

Although it was tedious, unending work, it was what the neighbors did and those people made up the Grange, Creamery Co-op, Masonic Lodge, and the churches. They were the elected officials in town, and work was part of our heritage.

It was the bond of helping and comforting each other in times of need or family sorrow. Without neighbors we wouldn't have had the volunteer fire department, country fair, square dances, skating parties, sleigh rides, quilting bees or church socials.

I'm grateful I was born in an era that exposed me to the down-to-earth fellowship of those people of character and integrity who appreciated the land, worked hard and felt a bond with the big-eyed horses and cows that seemed to understand when, in quiet moments, they were spoken to or called by name.

Those years on the farm ended abruptly for me and many other young men. World War II happened, and I spent the war years in the Army Air Corps. A short while after the war the farm stopped operating, and by then I was following other pursuits in the business world.

Many years ago, before the present owners, Susan and Harry Werner purchased the property, I went back to see what had happened to the old place: I was unprepared for what I saw and wrote a poem about my feelings.

The barns on Uncle Beach's farm long after the cows were gone.
W. S. Hart photo

Returning

I traveled today to the place of my youth,
Back to the old family farm;
I wanted to see what the changes would be
And if to me it still held charm.

It's been sixty odd years since I was boy
And saw the dirt road stretched so far,
But, today, I don't know why, I was surprised
To see it all covered with tar.

The meadow on the right has grown up to brush,
Tobacco barn nowhere in sight;
The only thing that's really just as it was
Is the house still standing there white.

The horse barn is also surrounded by weeds,
With the silo falling in, too.
The side hill has been allowed to grow back wild
Which shuts off the beautiful view.

The old weathered cow barn is filled now with junk,
The stanchions are empty and bare,
And there is a hint of the hay stored above
That used to smell sweet in the air.

The door on the milk house had slid off its tracks,
The whitewash all peeled and gray,
And no longer are milk cans set there to cool
As they were in happier day.

*   *   *

My Granby Drummer articles often concluded with nostalgic memory-jogging lists of sayings, brand names, smells, sights and other things that have passed from our daily experience. They are, in themselves, a trip down Memory Lane.

Sometimes I muse about the sights, sounds and other things that were prevalent in my youth but are few and far between today. Without any order I jotted down the following:

Katydids; fireflies; locusts; bumble bees; peepers; sounds from the frog pond like "knee-deep;" water running over the dam; flag root candy; horehound candy; licorice; elderberries; blackberries; spearing suckers; prohibition; hard cider; Moxie; homemade root beer; cutting brush to keep the pasture open; mending fence; forty-quart milk cans; Even-flow milk filters; white washing the cow barn and milk house; Griswold Salve; iodine; "Be Healthy Drink Milk" signs; the size of a hole dug to bury a horse or cow; cutting ice from the pond; ice house insulated with sawdust; no town snow plows; helping a calf being born; the whistle of a red tailed hawk; horses' hooves pawing a wood floor; the sharp, oiled clacking sound of a mowing machine cutting bar going back and forth; clicking of the hand mower when it was backed up; the sound of a stream of milk hitting the empty milk pail and changing to a heavier sound when the nearly full pail of milk frothed up; axe chopping in the distance on the next farm. Coon dogs baying in the woods; a hoot owl; the sound of a car crossing the loose planks on the old iron bridge at Silver Street; the high scream of a circular saw; chickens clucking while searching out the corn kernels in the barnyard; an iron-rimmed wooden wagon wheel grinding over dirt and loose stones; the squeal of the same wheel rubbing against the metal stop when the wheel was turned too far; the bawling of a calf; the mooing of a cow; the whinny of a horse; the softness of a horse's nose; a horse twitching its skin at the spot where a fly was biting; at milking time, squirting the ever present cat; the heavy sound of a felled tree; the sound of a scythe being sharpened on a grinding wheel and the sparks; the sound and feel of a whetstone being used on the scythe after cutting a long swathe; bacon sizzling and snapping in an iron skillet; the dull sound of eggs being whipped in a crockery bowl with a wooden spoon; the metal sound of the kitchen water pump; a farmer calling his cows with the time worn "come-boss, come boss;" playing a harmonica; harmonizing with my uncle in the evening.

GROWING UP IN
WEST HARTFORD

I was born in the second floor bedroom of a two-family brick house on Blue Hills Avenue in Hartford in 1922. My mother, a church soloist, sat up a few minutes after I came into this world and sang the doxology, "Praise God from whom all blessings flow." I wonder if in my teens, did she still feel the same?

My older sister Joan and me with our Grandfather Hart,
a Civil War veteran. W. S. Hart photo

In the slower 1930s, West Hartford was a relatively small town, and in my circle of friends everyone knew almost everything about everyone. I knew most of the parents in my neighborhood, and they tended to keep an eye on our activities. I remember, one evening doing something foolish down in the center. A neighbor walked by and said "Bill, your father wouldn't like to hear about this." West Hartford Center was very different from the busy place it is today.

We never forget

The marvelous retentive power of our minds always impresses me. The other day I happened to drive by the public airport in Simsbury where I saw several small private planes tied down by the runway. I also noticed the limp old-fashioned windsock waiting for a stirring breeze to fill it and show the wind's direction.

The still, quiet scene took me back to 1934, some 74 years ago, when I was 12 years old. It was then I had an opportunity to take my first airplane ride from Brainard Field in Hartford. The two-winged, single-engine plane had no resemblance to the sleek, shiny aircraft of today. Its wooden frame was covered with painted canvass. Its two cockpits were open to the sky and the varnished wood of the propeller glistened in the sunshine. Three guys from the neighborhood were with me.

As I recall, it cost $5 for the four of us to take a short flight. We sat in the front cockpit right by the big radial engine. It was a thrill to put my foot on a small step and climb first onto the wing surface and then lift my leg into the cockpit. That was also the first time I ever saw a seatbelt. It was awe inspiring to look sideways through the struts and wires holding the wings in place and then turn forward to see the big cylinder heads and spark plug wires in a circle just behind the propeller.

On the front wall of the cockpit were paper bags the pilot told us to use if we had to barf. He misjudged us; none of us had to use them. The pilot climbed aboard wearing a heavy jacket and a skintight leather helmet with his goggles hanging under his chin. He wore a white silk scarf tied around his neck. I later learned the pilots wore that silk to protect their necks against chafing from the constant turning of their heads against the jacket collar.

The pilot gave a whistle. A mechanic stopped his work in the nearby hanger and walked to the front of the plane. There were no electric starters in those days. The mechanic hollered "contact" and the pilot repeated the same word. At that instant the mechanic reached up with both hands, grabbed the top edge of the propeller, lifted his left knee to shoulder height, and with one strong jerk, pulled the propeller down. That action turned the engine over and it fired to life with a roar and a puff of black exhaust smoke.

Once the motor was wound up, the pilot raised his hand and the mechanic pulled the chocks from under the two wheels. The engine revved some more and we taxied to the long grass runway. There was some type of muffler on the motor, but it wasn't very efficient. It was almost impossible to talk with each other. We taxied to the end of the runway that let us take off into the wind. In the excitement of sitting so high from the ground with the deafening noise and the propeller whirling in front of me, I thought my heart would beat itself through my ribcage.

When the engine was at full power, the pilot released the brakes and we started down the runway. The ground whizzed by and the bumpy runway jolted my body. Just as quickly we were airborne and reaching for the sky. I watched the rounded roof of the hangar become smaller and smaller. Some people in small boats on the Connecticut River waved to us, which added to the excitement. It was great to fly over the Bulkeley Bridge, which we'd crossed getting to the airport. Later we circled around the Traveler's Tower and flew over the city. It was fun picking out buildings we knew and seeing the trolley cars turning to a stop at the Isle of Safety by the old State House.

The flight didn't last long, but I recall the sensation of the plane leaning left and right as the air currents lifted and moved the wings. We flew downwind parallel to the runway then made a quick left turn to line up heading into the wind. The engine was throttled back and the wind whistled through the wires by the struts. There were a couple of small bounces as the wheels touched down and we taxied back to the hangar.

I had no idea if I would ever fly again. I continued my young life doing the usual stuff as I grew up. Circumstance can change the moment, and without realizing it, I was nearly twenty years old when Pearl Harbor was attacked on December 7, 1941. We were all eager to enlist. I knew I didn't want to be a foot soldier so I enlisted in the Army Air Corps. My group was sent to Oswego, New York on Lake Ontario. It was there I learned to fly a single wing Piper Cub. The first ride down the runway was just as exciting as my ride in 1934. Actually, it was doubly thrilling, for now I was going to learn to fly and no longer be a spectator or a passenger.

That is all in the past and I don't care to fly any more, but I do appreciate the retentive power of my 85-year-old mind that lets me relive my youth in the early days of flying.

Today I get a thrill similar to flying when I throw my leg over my motorcycle, crank it up and head out on great country roads. I'm free again just as I was up in the air so many years ago.

A backward glance

This nonsense is directed at members of the over-the-hill gang who can relate to the 1930s. As I notice the male teenagers of today, I have a tendency to shake my head at some of their outfits. Other than wearing blue jeans, girls' attire hasn't changed much but the boys are something else.

I noticed two young guys walking by the house the other day. One reminded me of Spanky McFarland in the "Our Gang" movies. His cap was on backwards and his too-large sweatshirt extended to his thighs. His companion wore voluminous trousers with the crotch down near his knees. The pant cuffs collected in a bunch over his ankles and dragged the ground as he walked and the edges were frayed. Both boys sported heavy footwear that wasn't a sneaker, but an ankle high, boot-like affair that appeared to make it an effort to drag one foot after the other. I'm not being critical of today's youth. My generation's peer group identification certainly looked ridiculous to our parents.

Many of us wore white saddle shoes and argyle socks, and we rolled our pant cuffs up a few inches. I recall my father asking: "Where's the flood?"

In high school both sexes had a thing for what was called a "beer jacket." The jackets were made of an off-white lightweight canvass material and had brass buttons. They fell just below the waist and the fad was to cover them with your classmates' signatures.

Dressing for a date in my teens, I wore loose gabardine slacks with a herringbone sports jacket. Dark Cordovan shoes shined to a high gloss with Kiwi ox-blood-colored shoe polish enhanced the outfit.

The girls wore skirts and sweaters and bobby socks. Their shoes were usually loafers and the girls always pushed a nickel into the band across the instep so they could call home if a date became difficult.

Our hairstyles were not girl-like but were neat and trim to emulate the popular movie stars. Some of us wore a butch, brush-cut or crew cut; names for the same close-cut style.

For a while in junior high school I was considered a real "dude" because I wore the spats my father had stopped wearing years before. Dressed to kill, I took my date to the local cinema and treated her to such delicacies as Jujubes, Good & Plenty or a pack of Wrigley's Juicy Fruit, Black Jack or Beman's gum.

We all worried about our breath, so we gargled with Listerine or Lavoris before we left home and on a date depended on tried-and-true Sen-Sen.

I won't go into the music of that era, but I do recall my father asking me: "What the heck is a Flat Foot Floogie with a Floy-Floy?"

Today's casual dress code allows adults to go to fine restaurants and even church dressed the way I did when I went out to milk the cows.

There was a sense of pride in one's clothing until President John Kennedy's bare-headed style did away with men wearing hats. My first job after my discharge from WWII was at The Travelers Insurance Company as a Field Representative. I thought my attire was all right, but soon after I started the job I was told to let my brush cut grow, buy a dress hat and discard my sport jackets for suits.

Most men donned a soft felt fedora with a snap-style brim. Some bankers and executives went for homburgs with a rolled edge to the brim. These went well with a black chesterfield coat with velvet lapels that was set off by a white silk scarf.

I saved up and bought a real camel's hair polo coat and wore light-colored pigskin gloves. I thought I was quite jaunty when I took out a leather-covered cigarette case, tapped a cigarette on it to pack the tobacco down, and lit it with my silver Zippo lighter. I think that scene was copied from the suave actors of the day!

I miss the gallant days when men held doors open for women—and were thanked for it. It always made me feel important to tip my hat to a passing lady friend or remove it if we stopped to talk. Of course in those gentler times, women didn't go shopping in slacks, flat-heeled shoes and no makeup. Ah well, memories.

Our beautiful fall is back

I often think back to those falls during my high school days in the late 1930s that were the awakening of my adulthood. It was fun going back to school after working on my grandfather's farm in North Granby.

For the first few weeks sitting in a chalky smelling classroom, it felt odd to realize I no longer needed to awaken in the dark and help milk twenty cows by hand. The late summer rowens (second haying) was in the barn, and the corn harvested and blown into the big blue silo. I could even forget feeding the chickens and collecting the eggs. No more the daily chore of shoveling cow manure into the old spreader outside the barn door.

It was wonderful to get back in the school routine with the kids I'd known and shared memories with for so many years. It was also exciting to be with girls again.

The football team was getting into shape and learning complicated plays. The pretty cheerleaders were perfecting their routines. I can see and hear the school band practicing parade maneuvers with the leader thrusting a big baton in the air. The brass section struggled to read their music from a bobbing card attached to the horn in front of them. The poor guy lugging the base drum had my sympathy.

Those days were the end of the Depression years and I, not being very good at sports, went to work driving a delivery truck after school and on Saturdays. The job gave me a sense of accomplishment and, at twenty-five cents an hour, spending money.

Football games were played on Saturday afternoons, and I arranged my deliveries to drive by the game several times for a taste of the spontaneity and school spirit. I also liked watching the cheerleaders' high leaps and laughing faces as they spurred on the crowds' enthusiasm.

I figured I had an advantage on the football players. After each home game there was a dance in the gymnasium where I danced and laughed with the girls. The football guys were so beat from playing that they sat on the sidelines like zombies or didn't show up at all.

One bonus of driving a delivery truck was driving through town in autumn and watching the changing foliage in the neighborhoods and on the distant hills. It's not allowed today, but then the smell of burning leaves was one of the niceties of fall. The few remaining farms were buttoning up for winter, and roadside stands displayed orange pumpkins, sheaves of corn, fall flowers and red apples. Fresh cider was a seasonal treat.

In a few short weeks I'll admire this year's leaf display but somehow the atmosphere is different from those falls of long ago. No smell of burning leaves or the soft swish of a bamboo rake. Instead I'll hear the obnoxious sound of droning leaf blowers. The main difference is in my attitude. Years ago I was full of anticipation and expectation of the new world I was discovering. Now, as an old man, I reflect on the wars and trials of life my generation endured and the joys that certainly were there amidst the sadness.

My circle of friends is becoming smaller and smaller, giving the anticipation of fall and the coming winter a touch of nostalgia. I look to today's teenagers to carry on that exciting time of life when, for a while, the world is their oyster. I hope that my companion gray hairs also remember how lucky we are to have experienced the changing world that was so good to us.

If you don't believe me, think back to cutting wood for the kitchen stove, thawing out the water pump before it could be primed, shoveling a path to the barn with a wooden shovel, putting chains on the car, not having a car heater or windshield defroster, walking to school rather than being bused. I don't miss the crackly static on the old radio and I certainly don't miss digging those stupid potatoes.

I guess this old world ain't so bad after all.

What fun those days were

In August, I was sitting on my screened-in breezeway at just about dusk. Being somewhat nostalgic, I lit a small antique kerosene lamp and sat quietly listening to a classical music CD.

I was content in my calm reverie enjoying a small glass of Merlot. The evening was enhanced by the night sounds of katydids and tree frogs and an occasional blinking firefly completed the tranquility. It must have been the fireflies that carried me back to my teens in West Hartford.

It was a custom in June, when high school let out, for a bunch of us to go to the Connecticut shore and rent cottages for a week. There were usually enough kids so the girls had three cottages and the boys had three. We were fortunate to have teachers who were willing to act as chaperones.

As I recall, the girls had a curfew but not the guys. In that age of innocence only a couple of guys drank and they usually got sick. Mostly it was a week of good, clean fun—a poor man's version of Mickey Rooney and Ann Rutherford in the Andy Hardy movie series. A couple of the guys even had Model A Fords like Andy's.

We spent our days getting sunburned, swimming, playing some kind of beach ball and just lazing around. The big lure was dating the girls in the evenings. There were many happy beach parties with the blankets all spread in a circle around a fire of snapping, sparking driftwood. There was always a guy with a ukulele.

In our corny way, we sang the old favorites from our parents' era such as "There's a long, long trail a-winding into the land of my dreams . . ." Frank Sinatra hadn't hit it big yet but Bing Crosby tunes and Rudy Vallee's "Your Time Is My Time," played on a portable wind-up Victrola.

Without the music there was story telling, and a little later, quiet girl and boy talk. The background sounds of small waves on Long Island Sound blended perfectly with the moonlight sparkling on the water. Overhead were the stars of the Milky Way and, very rarely, someone shouted out "shooting star," and we all made a silent wish.

If we were lucky, we'd see the Long Island ferryboat going by with all its lights ablaze.

We weren't completely "goodie two shoes," for some of us smoked and did our best to do a little necking, which is a far cry from what I hear goes on today.

One night I didn't have a date and my friend, Joe Lewis, rode down from West Hartford on his Indian motorcycle. Joe and another friend wanted to see some of the shore's nighttime activities. Not being the "swiftest" guys around, the three of us piled onto the motorcycle and took off. When we came to the outskirts of a town like Clinton or Old Lyme, Joe had one of us get off, took the other guy through town, and came back for the other. We never got arrested. The ride went well and even now I recall the sound of that bike, the rush of wind, and see the yellowed headlight barely lighting up the winding blacktopped shore roads.

My musings are cut short as I hear the neighbor kid's booming bass speakers coming up the street two football fields away. Shortly, he and his pal will charge up on his "vram-vram, plang-plang-plang" motorcycle and with my tranquility completely shot, I'll be back to reality.

Winter, you've lost your punch

In the middle of raking leaves it hit me that winter is waiting, hat in hand, to make its presence known. I thought of last year and all the snow that everyone moaned about. My old brain started to churn and, in recollect, I decided we don't have it too bad today.

I have a self-starting snow blower and in a storm, the town's snowplows work around the clock to clear and sand the roads. Today, we don't even use snow tires. Years ago we crawled under the car and hooked chains and spreaders over the rear wheels, which was no fun in frigid weather. Invariably a chain link broke and it "wrap-wrap-wrapped" against the fender until you stopped and replaced it with a monkey link.

In the 1930s, West Hartford only had a couple of trucks that took a plow blade. In a heavy storm it took up to three or four days to clear all of the streets. The unemployed from Hartford were brought in to clear the sidewalks in the center of town. They shoveled the snow by hand, and threw it into town trucks that hauled it away and dumped it into Trout Brook.

Fortunately a trolley ran from Hartford to the Unionville section of Farmington. The Connecticut Car Company had huge plow blades mounted on work cars that kept the tracks clear so people were able to ride to work. Even when the side streets were impassable for a few days, we could trudge to Farmington Avenue and walk the tracks to the grocery store in the center.

When I was in old Hall High School and it snowed overnight, I listened to either Bob Steele or Ben Hawthorn (who was really Benton Hawthorn Deming) on the radio. They both announced whether or not the schools were closed.

When my buddy and I heard the schools were out, we grabbed our old metal snow shovels, and rang neighborhood doorbells to ask if we could shovel the walk. Sometimes we got lucky and were asked to shovel the whole driveway. That was quite a job because most of the wooden garages were at the rear of the property.

In the depression years, minimum wage was twenty-five cents an hour. If we shoveled from morning until dark, we each earned about five dollars for the day's work. My regular Saturday job at the grocery store paid two dollars and fifty cents for ten hours work, but with snow I made twice that amount.

Times have changed and so has winter clothing. We didn't have insulated gloves, jackets or L.L. Bean-lined boots to warm our feet. We were lucky if we had waterproof galoshes or arctics with metal buckles instead of laces. Sometime we wore "high-cuts" made of leather that came to just below the knee and had leather laces. The big selling point for these was the pocketknife that fit into a small pouch on the calf that closed with a metal snap. It didn't take long for high-cuts to become water logged and your feet felt frozen.

Today, kids ice skate in a heated indoor rink in their shirtsleeves. We went to the local pond and shoveled like crazy to clear the snow and oftentimes the underlying ice was very rough. It was a minor inconvenience that we didn't have shoe-skates. Instead we used skate blades that clamped onto our street shoes. I had weak ankles and the skates tended to flip-flop as I went across the ice. I was best at keeping the big fire going by the shore where we warmed up.

I do admit it was wonderful to skate on a bright, moonlight night under the stars and watch the aurora borealis in the north. Our breath hung in the air and the bursts of laughter were entirely spontaneous and carefree. An evening of skating always seemed much improved when I was with a pretty girl who laughed at my stupid stories and made me feel important.

I count my blessings that we have defeated the perils of winter, but I still like to reminisce about the labors of the good old days at the height of my innocent youth.

I never had it so good

The other afternoon, a big yellow oil truck pulled up out front. The driver climbed out, uncoiled a long umbilical cord from the rear of the truck and proceeded to pour liquid gold into my basement tank.

As I heard the whistling noise I thought of how the many gallons, at $2.39 each, were depleting my meager income. Well, being long-in-the-tooth, I thought back to those Depression years of the thirties when I was a know-it-all kid.

Our home's heating system preceded oil burners. We had coal delivered to our doorstep. A company in Hartford, some four miles away, sent blue anthracite coal out in a wagon pulled by a team of horses.

I can see it now. Two black men jumped down from the high wagon seat, carried a long metal chute to the rear cellar window and extended it down to the wooden bin by the furnace.

The coal came in big burlap bags, which the men slung over their shoulders and emptied them onto the chute. I can still hear the sharp tumbling noise of the coal as it slid out of sight, which created a lot of black dust that clung to the floor and rafters.

The coal didn't climb into the furnace by itself. It had to be shoveled by somebody, and I was usually elected. Each shovel full had to be spread evenly around the firebox, and at night, the fire was banked to assure live coals in the morning. To tend the fire properly, the grates were turned periodically, and the ash that dropped down was shoveled into metal ash cans that the town picked up each week. During the Depression money was tight, so the ashes went into a large barrel out back. We had a square screen-like box to sift unburned pieces of coal from the ashes.

As I watched the oil truck empty its stomach into my basement, I thought about how comfortable my little Cape house is. The building code requires insulation in the walls and attic floor. The doors have weather stripping, and double thermo-paned windows keep the cold out. They're so fancy I don't have to open the top or bottom and lean out to clean them. I push two buttons and the sash tilts inward so I can clean them from inside.

Way back, the old houses had no insulation and were not airtight. In winter, the window frames dried out and wind made them rattle. In summer, the dampness made them swell and stick shut. During freezing weather the old windows steamed up and, if cold enough, thin fern-like ice crystals formed on the inside. We scratched our names or made pictures in the ice with our fingernails.

Those old windows let a lot of air in because of the lose fit. Some smart guy came up with the idea of storm windows. They weren't made of lightweight aluminum with built-in screens like today. They were constructed of a wood frame with two large panes of glass. Those sashes were heavy. Each sash was numbered to correspond with the window it was made for. On the first floor level I installed them from the outside using a stepladder. Upstairs was the problem. I opened the lower half of the window and guided the storm sash through the opening and turned it upright. My adolescent arms were not that strong, which made it a chore to lean out and, without looking up, fit the eyelets at the top of the sash onto the hooks screwed into the upper window casing.

I recall, one very windy day, a storm sash almost got away from me. Fortunately, I didn't lose my grip entirely so it didn't smash to pieces on the ground. The sash tilted and hit the side of the house, breaking both panes of glass. That meant a trip to the hardware store where the clerk cut two panes of glass for me. At home, I installed small metal triangles to hold the glass in place, puttied around the edges to seal the glass in tight and painted the window to protect my repairs.

As you would imagine, my old man wasn't pleased with his protégé. If he'd scolded me I like to think I might have answered; "Don't be upset; after all you're ahead of the game because I'm the one who washes the windows and installs and removes the storm sashes. Also, I'm the one who keeps the furnace going and empties the ashes, mows the lawn, (with an iron push mower) and removes the snow with a heavy wooden-bladed shovel. And I do it for twenty-five cents a week."

Old-fashioned family discipline dictated that I may have had the thought, but would never have had the courage to say it.

How times have changed

I usually plan my activities well in advance but, because of circumstances, I was caught shopping during the final days of the Christmas shopping season.

It never occurred to me that the parking lot at the huge mall could be large enough to hold all the vehicles crowded in there. Inside the mall was an almost shoulder-to-shoulder crowd. I seriously doubt that the mall exercise walkers were doing their thing.

The building has two floors accessible by several wide escalators. While I was standing there being carried to the upper level, a comparison to the old days popped into my mind.

In the 1930s there were no malls in the suburbs, and there were no multi-lane thruways crowded with cars and eighteen-wheelers.

How simple it was to walk to the end of my street, board a trolley car and sit on a wide, varnished-straw seat watching the passing scenery and the people getting on and off.

When I was a tyke, Hartford was the shopping mecca for all of the outlying towns. It had several large department stores: G. Fox & Company, Steiger's, Brown Thompson's and Sage Allen's.

During the holidays the street posts were decorated and each store had cheerful displays in their windows. Salvation Army Santas stood on the street and at store entrances ringing their bells hoping for donations for the poor.

I was most interested in G. Fox & Company. When I was a kid my mother took me there shopping. She used her Fox's charge card or paid cash for each purchase. The sales slip, accompanied by the cash or charge card, was placed in a wire basket that was hoisted up on a wire-and-pulley system and carried to the cashier's department. Shortly, the basket returned with the receipt and change for a cash sale.

In later years, the baskets were replaced by a pneumatic system. The sales slip and the money or card were inserted into a flashlight-sized cylinder that was placed in a tube and whisked to a cashier.

The bank of elevators along the north side of the main floor was one of the most impressive things about G. Fox & Company Each car operator was outfitted in a snappy-looking uniform made up of a short vest and trousers and topped off with a hat with a shiny visor. A starter paced back and forth keeping an eye on the cars and the customers to keep things moving quickly. He held a small metal "cricket" in his hand, and just before the elevator was full, he pressed the clicker. The operator closed the elevator doors and away it went. As the car approached each floor, the operator called out the various merchandise displayed on that level letting passengers know where to get off.

I anticipated visiting Toyland on the tenth floor. When the elevator doors hissed open, a wonderland of bright and exciting toys awaited. My destination was the Lionel electric train display. Several trains ran around a complicated layout. I spent hours watching the passenger and freight cars speeding around and the engines tooting as they went through tunnels and stopped at the several stations.

Before my older sister told me there was no Santa Claus, I stood in the long line waiting to tell Santa what I wanted for Christmas. Of course I had to "fudge" a little and tell him I'd been a good boy.

Bill Hart, a train buff at age 7 in 1930. W. S. Hart photo

The years went by, and I went to G. Fox & Company as a teenager. By that time a restaurant called the Connecticut Room was the place to have lunch. While the women ate luncheon, they were treated to a fashion show. Those women went shopping wearing dresses, hats, heels and gloves that were a fashion statement of the times.

While I was in high school, the store initiated fashion shows for teenagers with local students for models. My girl friend, Mary Lee O'Brien, and I applied and were accepted as models for a couple of shows. One showcased eveningwear. Mary Lee was outfitted in a flowing ballroom gown, and I wore black tails similar to what Buddy Ebsen wore in the movies. I even had a collapsible top hat. We walked out on stage, and as the dance record started, I hit the hat with my hand to snap it open, and as we started to dance, placed it at a jaunty angle on my head. We whirled around the stage before walking the long narrow ramp through the center of the audience. It was wonderful. The audience of teenagers howled, whistled and clapped as we did our thing. That was probably the highlight of my adolescent years.

Where did the years go?

I recall, when I was a teenager, my dear mother saying: "Get the most out of life now for you, too, will be old someday."

These were idle words that I remembered through the years but suddenly, Wham! I am old. All the activities I took for granted are not so easy to do anymore.

A few years ago old George Burns sang a song with the then popular singer, Bobby Vinton. The words were something like "I know what it is to be young, but you don't know what it is to be old." Hmm, my mother's words have come home to roost.

My doctor tells me I'm in good health and my mind is okay. I tell him I'm concerned because I find myself doing little stupid things. I have to make out a shopping list otherwise I forget to buy the things I went to the store for. The problem is, sometimes I grab the shopping cart and realize I left the grocery list on the kitchen table.

The other evening while I was watching the boob tube, I felt like having a snack and decided to check out the refrigerator. A couple of minutes later I was standing in the bedroom wondering what I went in there for. Sure, my mind is fine! Some of my old fool companions say they have the same problem. It's interesting to me that I recall nonsense from grade school but last month takes a little memory jogging.

A while back, reminiscing about my teenage years, I realized what fun I had back in the 1930s. I'd hop on a trolley car and ride to Hartford for a movie, do some shopping or just wander around.

Those were the days of five-and-ten-cent stores such as W.T. Grant, Kresge's and Woolworth's. They had great lunch counters where you could buy a steamed hot dog and wash it down with a cold Hires root beer in a chilled mug.

Each store had a sheet music section and a lady to play the piano. You picked out some sheet music and she played it for you to help you make your selections.

Each store also had a record section. After picking through the racks, you took your selections to a small soundproof booth and played them to see which ones you wanted to purchase.

What a contrast with today. In our town we have almost an epidemic of teenage drinking, pot smoking, and drugs. The big thing is to throw a house party on a night when the parents will be away. The word spreads like wildfire, and during the evening the house overflows with partying kids. They spread out into the yard and into darkened automobiles where sex is prevalent.

The local police have raided several of these and arrested many of the kids. During one such raid, the parents were arrested for allowing underage drinking. They were put on trial and paid the penalties of conviction.

These young people in their baggy, peer-group clothing and body-part piercings probably refer to me as an old fogey. I said the same things about my parents when they weren't up with my times. Even so, it's too bad so many young people are following the blatant cultures of today and missing the wholesomeness we had in our awakening associations with the opposite sex.

As I said, "I know what it is to be young, but you don't know what it is to be old."

Was August Hot Enough?

When I was a teenager I thought farm work was hot, but in 1942, waiting to go into World War II, I worked at the Aetna in Hartford for one summer. A five and one-half-day workweek that paid $18.50.

There was no air-conditioning. All of the buildings' hundreds of windows stayed open in the hot weather. Days when the temperature remained in the upper eighties and low nineties, the buildings never cooled off at night.

In the office, the men wore ties and the women wore dresses. There were no short-sleeved sports shirts or slacks then. Adult men wore hats. In summer it was either a lightweight Panama or an off-white hard straw hat.

In a real heat wave, companies such as the Aetna, Travelers, Connecticut General, Phoenix and The Hartford let employees go home at noon. It helped, but the ride home in a hot trolley or in a car with the windows down wasn't pleasant.

I guess the point of this nonsense is to say that people born after 1945, when air-conditioning became more common in public places, have no idea of what it meant to experience a prolonged heat wave with no relief available.

My only regret is that my grandchildren will never experience how great it felt when you were covered with sweat and hay chaff, to dive into the old mill pond and cool off lying on your back, spouting clean, cold water into the air and looking up at the blue sky with white, puffy clouds floating by. Aaaah!

I miss the old telephone party line

My mother used to say, "You don't miss what you never had." The present generation takes so many things for granted that were miraculous inventions during my lifetime.

If only they could recall the first telephone. The telephone was patented in 1876 and at its inception, was a thing of wonder. I vividly recall the phone my Aunt Ethel had in Collinsville. It hung on the wall and looked like a wooden box with a black mouthpiece on the front and a receiver that hung from a hook on the side. Turning the hand crank on the right side contacted the operator.

To speak with somebody only a block away was magic; what we now take for granted had great meaning back then. Telephone service was available in some parts of Granby in 1896. Electricity didn't arrive until the 1920s.

It was a convenience for a customer to call the Loomis Brothers store and ask whether or not an article was in stock. That call saved hitching up the horse and wagon and driving some distance only to learn the item was out of stock. Think how it changed peoples' lives when in an emergency, help was only a call away.

In 1936, the telephone office was located on Hopmeadow Street in Simsbury. The switchboard identified each customer by a line number and a ring number; for example, Loomis Brothers Store was eight-ring-two.

When I was fourteen I was with my aunt and uncle in their 1928 Whippet when we stopped at the curb in front of the Simsbury exchange. The switchboard was on the second floor at the front, just over the main entrance. Aunt Marie called up to Helen, the operator on duty. Helen leaned out the open window and they chatted for a few minutes.

The operator was known as "central" and she knew the voices of the local phone users. You might ask for seven-ring-three and Helen would say, "Mary's gone to Hartford for the day, you'd better call tonight."

With several customers on each party line, news traveled fast because anyone could pick up and listen when they heard rings. They might even jump into the conversation.

One of my warmest teenage memories is of sneaking to the upstairs phone and talking sweet nonsense with the current love-of-my-life. It was always a worry when I heard a busy signal. Perhaps one of my rivals was listening to the mellifluous tones of my heartthrob and beating my time.

Another stupid memory goes back to the middle 1930s. A popular pipe tobacco, Prince Albert, was packaged in a red tin container. I admit, I actually called Kottedloff's Drugstore and asked if they had Prince Albert in a can. They said "yes," and I said, "Please let him out."

The once-so-friendly telephone has become a pest. I am plagued with telemarketers and unsolicited inquiries. When I call a business I get a recording telling me to punch this or that number on my touch-tone phone. While I wait to speak with a human, I'm subjected to a sales pitch or horrible music.

My pet peeve is calling a friend and hearing "We can't come to the phone right now." I have difficulty calling some people because they are on line with their computer, which ties up the phone line.

I am sorry some people are upset with me because I can't send or receive email. I have a few close friends with whom I correspond—on paper. It is a genuine pleasure to read a letter somebody sat down and pondered over; a letter written in no haste is full of deep thoughts.

My grandmother left diaries from 1875 to 1910, and through them I know how she thought and what went on in her household. When I receive a personal letter, I make a copy of my reply and attach it so that fifty years from now some family member can share the thoughts that were part of my life before they were born.

During those early years of Alexander Graham Bell's invention, it was a pleasure to answer the telephone.

A boy and his dog

It seems most towns of any size have a veterinary clinic or animal hospital. Some of them are quite expansive and include kennels for boarding and special grooming services. The clientele appears to be from the upper income groups. Even the dogs look a little snooty with their in-vogue hair clippings and independent attitudes.

Many of the animals are foreign to me, and I can't pronounce some of the breed names. What I notice most, probably because of their absence, are mongrels or what we used to call mutts. Back in the 1930s we'd see an occasional pedigreed dog but most were mixed breeds.

When I was fourteen and living in West Hartford, somebody gave me a mutt that was a cross between a Cocker Spaniel and a Dachshund. It was odd looking but smart and affectionate. I named her Brownie. I taught her to sit, roll over, fetch, and when I said, "speak," she barked for me. Brownie greeted me eagerly, and licked my hands when I came down to the kitchen at four in the morning prior to starting my Hartford *Courant* paper route. She followed me to each doorstep and was great company on those lonely and cold mornings.

In those days, West Hartford didn't have the snow removal equipment they have now and it might be two or three days before the side streets were plowed. Many a morning, Brownie's and mine were the first footprints down those quiet roads.

The paper cost three cents, and I received one cent for delivering it. If the customer paid the *Courant* direct I received half of a cent. I had to complete the route each weekday by six a.m. and eight a.m. on Sunday.

I worked many hours to earn very little money. After school, I made a weekly visit to each customer to collect for the paper. Often it took several call backs to catch a person at home. Each week I sat with the *Courant* supervisor and settled my account.

At the time I thought I was doing something important. With a route of some fifty customers, I made about three dollars and fifty cents a week, which made me feel independent. I recall my parents telling me the paper route was character building.

Today, a man sitting in a warm van with his radio on reaches out and tucks the paper into a plastic receptacle at the curb.

When I came home after school Brownie ran around me and jumped up, beside herself with joy. For some reason my parents had her tail cut off so it was only about three inches long, which didn't seem worth wagging.

About this time, I was spending some of my summer vacation on the family farm in North Granby. Brownie couldn't go with me because she chased the chickens, the cows and the horses: it just didn't work.

On one occasion, after several days away from home, I returned to learn my mother, apparently out of compassion, had given my dog to a young polio victim who lived in Collinsville. The kid was Oakie Strout, a nice guy who was about my age. I used to spend time with him when I visited my Aunt Ethel who was his next-door neighbor.

I was crestfallen, and couldn't believe my mother had given my beloved companion away. Immediately on hearing this, I jumped on my bike and pedaled from our house, near West Hartford center, to Oakie's on the other side of Collinsville; about ten miles each way. I picked up Brownie and sat her in the wire basket attached to the handlebars and returned home. I still remember how crushed I was by that experience.

One day, shortly after, I was riding my bike on Farmington Avenue. As I neared home, I saw Brownie, way up ahead, chasing a neighbor's dog that she played with. The pair were trotting across the trolley tracks, and I saw a passenger car approaching. The first dog got by all right, but the car couldn't avoid Brownie and ran over her.

I was struck with horror when I saw my pal writhing in pain and making loud yelping sounds in the middle of the road. 1 threw my bike down and ran to her, picked her up and carried her to the embankment by the roadside.

I must have sounded crazy to the people around me because, as her eyes turned upwards in her head, and she died, I kept repeating, tearfully, "speak to me Brownie, speak to me."

The couple in the car that struck her stopped and came back. It must have been a terrible experience for them to view the scene, hear my words, and know they were part of the tragedy.

Swingin' with the Big Band Era

This essay is for seniors who miss the calmer days of music. Back in the day, we bought sheet music and 78-rpm records at the five and dime store and listened to juke boxes on our dates. The world of the Big Bands and their singers was fascinating and we each had our favorites. Some of us tried to imitate various singing styles.

I've spoken with today's youth who are into popular music that is very different from the gentle melodies of our generation. They mention names of current singers, but I don't recognize any of them. Today, popular music shows are held in huge arenas with flashing lights, glitter and ear-damaging speakers. Most of the songs consist of a couple of words that are repeated incessantly. These shows often end up with drug busts and fights.

The dancing I see is not a couple holding each other, but some type of gymnastics with arms and legs flailing around and heads flopping from side to side. Some of the hip movements parallel those of the stag films I've seen at bachelor parties. Most of the dances we went to ended with the band quietly playing "Good Night Ladies."

As you read further, perhaps you'll remember dates you had—a high school prom, dancing at a road house, a lakeside or seaside pavilion or just a wind-up portable phonograph at a beach party by a log fire under the stars.

You may recall how the Big Bands came to a nearby city and you saw and heard your favorites in person. My biggest thrill was seeing Frank Sinatra with Tommy Dorsey when they came to Hartford. These old bands traveled the country by train and bus and were on the road most of the year. There was no television; you had to be there in person.

I think back to Benny Goodman, Tommy and Jimmy Dorsey, Cab Calloway, Duke Ellington, Count Basie, Bunny Barrigan, Artie Shaw, Blue Baron, Frank Chatsfield, Percy Faith, Russ Morgan, Enoch Lite, Milton

DeLugg, Bobby Hackett, Mitch Miller, Rudy Valee, Charlie Spivak, Phil Harris, Bob Crosby, Stan Kenton, Tony Pastor, Louis Prima, Shep Fields, Guy Lombardo, Kay Kyser, Ozzie Nelson, Sammy Kaye, Harry James, Freddy Martin, Glenn Miller, Lawrence Welk, Horace Hite, Louis Armstrong, Les Brown, Vaughn Monroe and Fred Waring.

I remember the guys who sang: Andy Williams, Bing Crosby, Nat King Cole, Frank Sinatra, Russ Columbo, Mel Torme, Billy Eckstein, Vic Damone, Sammy Davis, Jr., Dean Martin, Tony Bennett, Perry Como, Frankie Lane, Dick Haymes, Al Jolson, Eddie Cantor, Dick Powell, Jimmy Durante, Johnny Ray, Fred Astaire, Gene Kelly, Al Martino, Gordon McRae, Eddie Fisher, Julius Larosa, Tony Martin and Lanny Ross.

Once the guys started traveling with the bands, the girls got into the act: Patty Paige, Connie Boswell, Helen O'Connell, Jo Stafford, Peggy Lee, Doris Day, Dinah Shore, Jane Powell, Ella Fitzgerald, Lena Horne, Sarah Vaughan, Kate Smith, Eartha Kitt, Mary Martin, Jeanette MacDonald, Kathryn Grayson, Judy Garland, Frances Langford, Ann Murray, Harriet Nelson, Margaret Whiting, Gisele McKensie, Rosemary Clooney, Ginger Rogers, Helen Forest, Theresa Brewer, and "Lilton" Martha Tilton.

All these bands and singers had their own renditions of songs such as: "I'll Never Smile Again," "Sunday Monday or Always," "I Love You Truly," "Moonlight Serenade," "Unforgettable," "Night and Day," "Stardust," "The Way You Look Tonight," "Love Walked In," "As Time Goes By," "The Man I Love," "Quiet Nights," "Rosalie," "You Made Me Love You," "Surrender," "Moonlight Becomes You," "Don't Fence Me In," "Three Little Words," "Love Letters," "Blue Skies," "Marie," "Mona Lisa," "In The Still Of The Night," "A Foggy Day," "I Surrender Dear," "Embraceable You," "Maybe" and "Little White Lies."

In 1943, I was stationed at Oswego, New York with the Army Air Corps. I was twenty years old when I met Phyllis, who was nineteen. We thought of getting married, but it didn't pull together. Our song was "Sunday, Monday or Always." Fate works in mysterious ways, and these many years later we are together again. We've settled on our song—"We're Almost There."

WORLD WAR II

Was it really that long ago?

Memorial Day is upon us and I've been thinking about the guys I grew up with who didn't make it back from World War II. Those thoughts took me back to my service during the war years; the years that changed life for my generation.

I was nineteen, and in my first year at Trinity College in Hartford when Pearl Harbor was attacked on December 7, 1941. As the winter wore on, I realized my being drafted was inevitable.

In the spring of 1942, the U.S. Army Air Corps mounted an advertising drive to recruit Aviation Cadets. A college degree or an equivalent was required to qualify; the latter required passing a daylong written exam.

I didn't want to be drafted and become a foot soldier, marching all of the time and sleeping on the ground. It was more intriguing to picture myself flying P-47 fighter planes wearing goggles, a leather jacket with a white silk scarf wrapped around my neck and streaming out behind.

The propaganda said I could go to flight school, become a pilot and receive a commission as a Second Lieutenant. Imagine what that prospect did to a nineteen-year-old kid?

I applied and spent a day in an old building near the railroad station in Hartford taking the tests. Low and behold, this uneducated guy passed the darn thing and was enlisted in the program.

My buddy Butch, who lived a few doors away, wanted to join but was scared stiff about the exam. The day after I was accepted, with all of the stuff still fresh in my mind, I told Butch all about the questions and he passed.

Several weeks later I was playing touch football, and separated my shoulder where the clavicle attaches to the upper arm. I had surgery at

Hartford Hospital, and that held me up for a couple of months. Ironically, my pal Butch was my alternate. He went in my place and eventually became a B-24 bomber pilot stationed in the South Pacific for over two years.

The day of my induction I took a special train to Fort Devens, Massachusetts. Our group was a mishmash of other innocents from all walks of life. I was wearing a light brown pinstripe suit and a tie.

At Fort Devens we signed in and got GI haircuts that resembled a brush-cut or flattop. We spent three days learning to march without falling all over each other—in our civilian clothes. We didn't get uniforms until we arrived at Atlantic City, New Jersey, for basic training.

On the fourth day we arrived in Atlantic City. The big hotels had been taken over by the Air Corps. We were assigned to the Claridge Hotel where our room was on the twelfth floor. It had been stripped of its carpeting, drapes and furniture. Six double bunks sat on bare concrete floor. Twelve soldiers lived in one room.

In the formerly beautiful dining room, which had been gutted to become the mess hall, we took three meals a day. We weren't allowed to use the elevators. We climbed or descended twelve flights of stairs several times a day.

A pip-squeak PFC (Private First Class) was in charge of our floor and had a desk at the end of a long corridor. When we saw him, he required us to stand at attention, salute and call him "Sir." To fill our free time, he made us memorize the Army's General Orders, which spelled out a soldier's responsibilities.

We were called Aviation Students, and the recruiting program allowed regular Army people to transfer into the program if they qualified. Because they had some military experience, they became the officers of our squads or flights. My flight's corporal seemed to enjoy his new position of authority.

After breakfast and cleaning the quarters, we went down twelve flights of stairs to a courtyard and fell in for close order drill. The corporal liked to look up at the sky and say, "It looks like rain. Go get your rolled raincoats." Another trip up and down twelve flights! After a while, he brought us to a halt, and the dear man said: "It looks like I was wrong, it's not going to rain so take your raincoats back to your quarters." The stairs became part of our lives.

I was a wise guy, and, one day when we were marching, I made some remark to my buddies about how "chicken" the corporal was. He stopped the drill, called me front and center, and said "Since you can't keep quiet, take two laps around the hotel complex." Being a wise guy, I said, "Sir, the General Orders we memorized say you can't ask a man to do anything you wouldn't do yourself, so let's go." A hesitant look covered the face of this fledgling corporal before he finally hollered: "Get back into ranks and shut up." Why didn't my bluffs work that well when I was playing poker?

In the mess hall we quickly learned not to take more than we could eat. As you left the hall what remained on your tin tray was scraped into a trashcan. MPs with billy clubs stood guard over those cans and they made you eat any leftovers that were edible.

The Air Corps recruiting program was so successful that there was a backup at every training field. To correct the problem, the Corps set up College Training Detachments where we studied things like math and physics. I was sent to a college in Oswego, New York for three months.

The airfields were still full. Our group went to Fort Myers, Florida, took training and received Aerial Gunner's wings. The pilot schools still were not ready for us, so we went to navigation school at Ellington Field in Houston, Texas. It was there I received my wings as a Second Lieutenant Navigator and was assigned to B-17 bombers. I became part of a flight crew that was sent to Sioux City, Iowa, for six months training for flying in fifty-ship formations and making simulated bomb runs.

At last we were ready to go overseas. We were scheduled to take off late one night, and I was in the flight room doing some last-minute course corrections for our flight to Italy. I looked up and saw a sergeant erasing our plane number from the departure board. I asked him what was going on and he said: "We just got the orders. No more B-17s are going to Europe—the war is over—over there."

After we sobered up, we were assigned to a section of Air Transport Command to ferry planes between air bases. Finally, we were slated to go to B-29 training out of Tampa, Florida. The day we stepped off the train the city was in a state of celebratory pandemonium. The war in Japan had ended that day.

I felt as though I was the most trained person in the Air Corps and, after all was said and done, I never fired a shot.

I was married in February 1949, and we spent two days of our honeymoon at the Claridge Hotel in Atlantic City where I had lived with eleven other guys at the beginning of my training. It gave me great pleasure to call room service and order breakfast in bed for two under very different circumstances.

Bill in U.S. Army Air Corps dress uniform in 1944.
W. S. Hart photo

Everything in its time

I recently wrote an article about my service in World War II assigned to a flight of B-17 Flying Fortress bombers. I've been thinking about that again and thought maybe I'd expand on one portion of it.

I was stationed at Sioux City Air Force Base. For the first several weeks, training concentrated on the pilots gaining confidence in close-formation flying in a three-tier, fifty-ship configuration. It took skill to keep a four-engine bomber in tight proximity to another as it bounced around in the air currents created by the wind and prop wash from the other B-17s. Flying that closely together it was possible to lip-read what a crew member in the next plane was saying. During these maneuvers P-39 fighter plane pilots practiced strafing runs on the formation.

Once pilots were proficient in formation flying, they zeroed in on the real purpose of the training: pinpoint bombing practice on simulated German industrial targets so that we could blend in with the squadrons already in action out of England.

In the first phase of training, the crew just went along for the ride. The bored enlisted men got on the intercom and hollered, "Hey lieutenant, how about some music?" I'd tune in a local radio station and they happily listened to the music of Tommy Dorsey and Glenn Miller through their earphones.

In the early training we didn't carry any fake bombs so the bomb bay was outfitted with a spare gasoline tank to increase the range of the aircraft. On one training mission, five more planes were needed to fill out the fifty-ship formation. Our crew was called. However, we didn't have extra tanks in our bomb bays. We took off on a cold winter morning, and at altitude, it was twenty or thirty below zero. You have no idea how cold you could get just sitting there. I beat the system. I removed the electric cover from the Norden Bombsight, put my feet inside, drew the drawstring tight and my feet were warm as toast.

We didn't plot a course on those missions. The purpose was to sharpen the pilot's skills by making random turns all over the sky. If we wanted to find out where we were, we used the Radio Directional Finder (RDF). In addition, each navigator had an RDF map for each state. By entering the frequency of a radio station, its relative bearing showed up on a circular compass display. Bearings for three surrounding stations were plotted on the RDF map. The point where the lines intersected identified the plane's location. With that position, you could plot a course to any location you desired.

On one particular day, after logging the required hours of practice, it was time to return to base. However, the RDF units were giving multiple false bearings. Panic set in—fifty airplanes flying in tight formation and nobody had any idea of where we were. We later learned that we'd flown over North Dakota where the magnetic field from iron ore deposits interfered with the radio transmissions.

We all carried contact maps that were like a road map with more details including towns, rivers, lakes, mountains and airfields. The pilots, navigators and bombardiers huddled over those maps. Adding to the confusion, we were flying in a light snowstorm and the ground was covered with snow. The lakes and small streams were frozen over, and with snow cover, were indistinguishable. No one had a clue as to his position. Suddenly we spotted a river and decided to follow it in hopes of identifying a landmark. The Des Moines River eventually led us to Des Moines itself.

The planes with extra tanks broke off and headed back to Sioux City. Five planes were too low on fuel to make it to home base. We landed at the Des Moines airport. One bomber had a problem.

During landing, the flight engineer stood between the pilot and copilot, and used his throat mike to call off the airspeed to the pilot. Without knowing the airspeed, you can undershoot or overshoot the landing area. Airspeed was registered on the instrument panel from a Pitot tube that projected from under the nose of the plane. A cloth sleeve placed over the tube when the ship is on the ground prevents blowing dirt from getting into it. During preflight inspection someone had failed to remove the cover.

The B-17 was just ahead of us, and we watched its landing attempt. It approached too fast, overshot the end of the runway and headed for a stand of trees. It was not going to stop soon enough. At the last minute the pilot ground-looped the plane to the right. The huge tail assembly swung around onto the uneven grass surface alongside the runway and the rear landing gear snapped off. Fortunately the plane was off the runway, and we were able to land.

We left our ships, and entered the control tower where we learned that Des Moines was a training center for newly inducted WACs, formally designated the Women's Army Auxiliary Corps (WAAC). The crews were in a state of euphoria. All in our early twenties, we were lonely for female companionship and here was a city full of young WACs we hoped were lonesome for male companionship. Wow! What a place to get stranded. Unhappily the powers that be saw the hazards in that. While we were fed in the local mess hall, they had our B-17s gassed up and sent us back to Sioux City.

You can imagine the stories we told back at base about what could have happened had we been let loose in that land of opportunity in Des Moines. I guess life is made up of what-might-have-beens.

Memory lane is a nice address

An old carton of letters jogged my memory of more trying times during WWII. In my small community, planning and teaching volunteers for the Air Raid Warning System was serious business. Wardens wore identifying clothing with armbands and white helmets; each warden carried a flashlight and a whistle and drew watches from darkness until dawn. The lookout places on the roofs of a few tall buildings and the mountaintops were miserable in cold, windy or wet weather. Hot coffee was a welcome and necessary staple.

Just before I was inducted, I recall hearing loud siren warnings. All public lights were extinguished and vehicles had to stop and shut the lights off. Wardens patrolled the neighborhoods to assure that houses had blackout shades pulled down. If a sliver of light showed, a loud whistle alerted the wrongdoer.

On the home front, there were shortages. Rationing stamps applied to gasoline, tires, food and some clothing items. Women were urged to go into the work force to replace men who had enlisted. Every town held scrap metal drives, and women organized to roll bandages. Organizers of dances and entertainment for transient soldiers often recruited eligible girls to attend those functions. Many couples met at a canteen or dance and found romance while others became good pen pals.

Women and girls had a problem. Silk, and even newly introduced nylon stockings were almost nonexistent. Both fibers were needed for parachutes and other war goods. The cosmetic industry saved women's dignity by inventing leg paint. To achieve the real stocking look of the day, they drew a thin black seam up the backs of their legs with a pencil. That was fine unless they were caught out in the rain.

In 1942, chromium use for the military forced auto manufacturers to eliminate chrome trim and use other materials for bumpers. The next year, new car production ceased as factories began turning out war equipment. It became a problem for car owners to keep their older cars in running order. Tire rationing was implemented to encouraged citizens to limit travel and gasoline use. New rubber tires were rationed and hard to find. The use of recapped and re-grooved tires was encouraged until they too went on the rationing list in 1942.

Food rationing forced many to grow Victory Gardens and bring the old Bell or Mason jars out of storage. Homegrown vegetables were delicious, but there was a shortage of butter. Margarine, which had been around since the 1800s and looked like white lard, took its place. By law, manufacturers couldn't color the stuff, so a capsule of yellow liquid in the package was blended in at home.

There was no TV, FM radio or stereo sound. Speakers didn't have bass and treble controls and the sound was full of static. Radio stations faded in and out. However, evening radio broadcasts brought the day's war news into most homes. The morning newspapers and magazines filled in the details.

All was not lost in the war effort; there were some good times. Big bands cranked out patriotic and romantic records for the troops and the people at home. The movie industry turned out nostalgic pictures about hometowns and mom and apple pie. News clips at the beginning of each show in the theater brought the battlefront home. War movies hit their stride and glorified the men in various services and fields of battle.

Some of us laughed at the fake battle and flying scenes. For example, B-17 bomber crews used an intercom system to communicate because the un-muffled roar of four Wright Cyclone engines was deafening. Without the intercom, you put your lips right up to a person's ear and shouted. Even that close, the message might have to be repeated several times. By contrast, in the movies, handsome Van Johnson played a bomber pilot, and without a headset, he easily spoke to his co-pilot and hollered down to the navigator and bombardier in the nose section. Flyers in the theater hooted at that mistake.

The almighty dollar was king, and cigarette companies capitalized on the war effort. In 1942, the American Tobacco Company changed the Lucky Strike brand packaging from dark green and gold to white with red trim. Radio Advertising played up the change with the slogan—"Lucky Strike Green Has Gone to War"—suggesting that the change supported the war effort by freeing the green dye for the war effort. Listeners disliked the slogan and it was dropped from broadcasts sponsored by Lucky Strike.

I feel sorry for Korean and Vietnam-War era soldiers and the people at home. The country wasn't involved and fully behind them as it had been during World War II. They didn't experience the public's enthusiasm for the efforts of women in wartime; they didn't sing that uplifting song, "Rosie the Riveter" or root for the WACs, Waves and WAAFs (Woman's Auxiliary Air Force).

In my memory, I dwell on the good times I had in service and think of the warmth of the fine people I met. Many guys didn't come back and others were disabled. Time goes by, and that generation of soldiers is rapidly passing on. Some of us cherish good memories of that time when there was some semblance of civility to the slaughter of war that was totally unlike the present-day horror of people blowing themselves up to kill innocent civilians.

Come fly with me

From my picture window I watch airliners as they approach Bradley Field in Windsor Locks. Sometimes, way up above, I can make out the contrails of other jets making their ways across country.

I have no desire to be up there, because to me, they aren't flying; they're sitting in a living room with all of the comforts of warmth, television, food and drinks. For me, real flying goes back to World War II when I was assigned to B-17 Flying Fortress bombers. The four Wright Cyclone engines had no mufflers and the sound was deafening because the aluminum-skinned aircraft had no soundproofing insulation.

Those old planes had no heat. We wore sheep-lined leather jackets and boots. Removing your heavy gloves was dangerous. As the plane gained altitude, the temperature dropped two degrees for every thousand feet. If the ground temperature was twenty degrees, it was thirty-five degrees below zero at twenty-five thousand feet. Remember when you were a kid and touched your tongue to the sled runner, it stuck there for a minute? Well, touching metal at altitude had the same result.

My interest in flying goes back to when I was five years old in 1927, when Charles Lindberg flew his Spirit of St. Louis across the ocean. My heroine, Amelia Earhart, also flew the Atlantic in 1928. I followed the flights of Wiley Post who flew the world with his pal Will Rogers. They were killed in a crash in 1935 at Point Barrow, Alaska. Also of that generation, the amusing pilot known as "Wrong Way Corrigan" flew the Atlantic without permission because of his navigational error in bad weather. As a result, he flew from New York to Ireland rather than following his flight plan, which listed his destination as Long Beach, California.

In grade school I built model airplanes out of balsa wood and covered the airframes with tissue paper. A wound-up rubber band turned a small propeller to power the two-winged craft. It took several hours to build one of those things. I recall gluing a fuselage together and putting it on the radiator to dry overnight. In the morning, it was scattered in small pieces all over the floor. My dog liked the taste of the balsa. He'd chewed it up and spit it out.

When I was 12, three friends and I pooled five dollars to pay for an airplane ride from Descomb Flying Service at Brainard Field in Hartford. The old canvass-covered bi-plane had two open cockpits; the one in front held four people. We flew around the Traveler's Tower and down the Connecticut River to Middletown and back.

Years went by, and Pearl Harbor came on December 7, 1941. We were at war. I knew the draft was inevitable and decided I'd rather fly than be shot at on the ground. I joined the U.S. Army Air Corps.

World War II was so different from the war in Iraq. It was a total war effort that engaged everyone in the country. I was excited about being called up and leaving my small town as part of a grand effort to save our way of life. Everyone was dedicated to defeating Germany and Japan.

When I turned twenty, I was assigned to an airfield in Texas where we practiced nighttime celestial navigation using a sextant just as the old mariners did when they took fixes on the stars to find their way. One night we were flying in a twin-engine aircraft with its passenger section set up as a classroom. We'd taken off under an overcast sky and climbed until we broke out on top at some eight thousand feet. It was spectacular to see the bright moon and shining stars overhead. Beneath us, the cloud layer was silvery and bright and seemed to extend to infinity. Like most guys at that tender age, I thought I was invincible and no harm could come to me; I'd live forever.

Pow! That belief was challenged in a split second as red and orange flame poured out of the left engine. The copilot hit the fire extinguisher button but nothing happened. After a few minutes the pilot ordered us to get into our chutes and stand by the escape hatch ready to bail out. On that flight we had chest chutes that looked like small, rolled up sleeping bags. Large metal clips secured the chute to the harness we wore on every flight.

We stood by the hatch looking into the vast darkness and watched smoke blowing by the opening. To this day I can't believe how calm I felt. Something within me reasoned that it was better to chance jumping into the unknown than staying with a plane that might crash or blow up at any minute.

We'd been exposed to basic parachute techniques by jumping from an eight-foot-high platform. We were taught to land on both feet, make a forty-five degree turn to the right, do a somersault on our right arm and shoulder and come to our feet.

I couldn't wait to get out of that plane! Then, just as suddenly as the flame had appeared, the extinguisher kicked in and the fire was out. Whew! We limped back to base on one engine and landed without a problem.

The training we went through focused on putting together a ten-man flight crew that could competently operate a B-17 bomber. Each member developed his own expertise as a pilot, navigator, bombardier, radioman, flight engineer or machine gunner. Over the months of training the crew became a family, and each member supported and protected the others.

A crew remained intact through stateside training and became a fighting unit in England as part of a huge armada of bombers performing precision daylight raids over industrial targets in Germany. In the States, many B-17 and B-24 training fields simulated the overseas flying conditions. Coordinated air strikes don't just happen, they have to be planned and practiced. Our crew went to Sioux City, Iowa where we started training in earnest.

By six in the morning on a typical day, we were on the flight line where enlisted men prepared the planes for flight. The officers gathered in the auditorium where we were briefed on the day's mission. As navigator, I plotted the course on my maps, figured fuel consumption and gathered information on any weather conditions that could affect our flight.

At the airstrip, our ship lined up with 49 other B-17s and prepared for takeoff. Once in the air, we rendezvoused at a designated area, and formed into a fifty-ship, three-tiered formation. The lead navigator set a course for a "turning point" where the formation pivoted and went in a straight line to the target.

In the vast barren areas of Iowa, bull's-eye targets covering several acres spread out below us. The targets represented German industrial sites and our job was to drop our bombs on the targets. The bombardier used a Norden Bombsight and in the last few minutes of the run, he controlled the aircraft. We watched the black-powder-filled bombs drop and waited for the puffs of smoke that marked where they'd hit.

While we were on a bomb run, fighter pilots trained in attack maneuvers dove through our fifty-ship formation. Our 45-caliber machine guns were equipped with cameras, and after we landed the pictures were used to improve the gunner's accuracy. It was a dangerous training game. On average we lost three, ten-man flight crews a month through mechanical failures or training errors.

Looking back, it's difficult to believe that as a twenty-year-old, I was involved in such a huge and well-coordinated program. I'm still impressed with what we accomplished 65 years ago with that equipment.

The problems and uncertainties of flying those old bombers was "raw" flying. It just can't be compared to a joy ride in a supersonic jet of today.

Drop me a line

What a shame the average person doesn't write letters anymore. Today it's mostly email and faxes that look mechanical and have no hint of warmth from the human touch. A handwritten letter has so much more character that, over time, may give someone insight into the persona of the writer. In the years to come those electronic messages will have no nostalgia connected to them. They will just be cold copies.

On the other hand, I have letters written over 60 years ago during World War II. I also have many written by my grandmother in the late 1880s. It's a generation thing. In the early 1940s most people took a pen in hand because few knew how to type or couldn't afford a typewriter. In my closet is a special box that contains all the letters my mother sent me during the war years of 1942 to 1945, when I was in the Army Air Corps. In another box are letters from other relatives, classmates and, of course, some old girl friends.

In the present world of openness and freedom to say most anything of a personal nature, these old letters might be boring to my teenage grandchildren. To me, those letters were lifelines to the hometown I'd left behind. As I read them now, they seem rather dull even to me. But then it was interesting to learn that Mrs. Sturtevant's cat "Winnie," had died, or Great Aunt Fanny had the gout or the neighbor down the street got drunk and lost his false teeth.

It was through this correspondence I learned of the death of a boyhood friend who had gone overseas. The worst was to learn about a pal being blinded or losing an arm or a leg. I looked forward to receiving addresses for guys overseas so I could drop them a line. I also found out about the girls' war efforts with volunteer work and entertaining soldiers at the local dances.

In small talk with today's younger generation, I've learned that they don't write letters to anyone. They use the computer or whip out a cell phone and send pictures back and forth. I guess I'm really out of it. I feel these kids are missing something. Even in my dotage I recall the wonderful exchanges of pure affection those old letters contained. None of those romances were serious, and we were caught up in the aura of the times. We had no idea whether we'd have a normal future of marriage and kids. The possibility of not returning from the war dwelt heavily on our young minds. Those innocent, semi-intimate exchanges with the opposite sex opened up unexplored areas of thinking that were welcome. I realize I'm probably on a little different wavelength from many old coots, but I still fondly recall those warm thoughts from young hearts.

Mail call was a daily event at some bases where I was stationed. I was writing full time to one dear girl, and I couldn't wait to receive her letters. She drenched her letters with perfume. On one airfield we had a wiseacre corporal who was Company Clerk, and he liked to have fun handing out the mail. When he called out a name the soldier came forward for his mail. This corporal always took my letters, held them to his nose, fluttered his eyelids and made some suggestive remark about the contents. I got kidded a lot.

At that time, letters went beyond the instant of happiness when they were first read; they were stored in my footlocker and in down moments, they lifted my spirits. Many lonely nights were made more bearable by re-reading those letters. Once in a while I received snapshots from some of the guys and girls. Often they'd been taken in a self-operated booth at the local five-and-dime store.

In my declining years, I often pull out some of the dog-eared letters and relive the emotions of those oh-so-gentle years of youth. The years before I became involved in the adult problems of family, kids and work that overcome us all. How special to shed a present problem and quietly turn back life's pages to the years when the world was our oyster.

Why not take a few minutes and drop somebody a line?

Revisiting "Padiddle"

Back in July of 2006, I was looking through a magazine dedicated to the memories of World War II. A letter to the editor gave a short description of the game of "Padiddle." It only scratched the surface.

In 1943, I was stationed at Oswego, New York. The local teachers college held a dance for servicemen and I danced with a pretty coed. I found the courage to ask her for a date and she accepted. That first Saturday night we walked quite a distance to the center of town where there was entertainment. It was dark and, in a shy way, I asked Phyllis if she had ever played "Padiddle." She had never heard of it so I explained. If she saw a car with only one headlight on she could slap me. However, if I saw it first I got to kiss her. We laughingly started out and I let her spot a couple of cars with only one light. She jokingly gave my face two light slaps.

It was amazing how many old cars had only one light during the war. I quickly spotted two with only one light. I didn't press for my reward and we continued our evening out. When we returned to her sorority house, we sat on the porch for a while and I reminded Phyllis she had fulfilled her part of the game by slapping me but she still owed me two kisses. She was nineteen, and I was twenty, and we were rather inexperienced. She reluctantly let me have two quick kisses. We enjoyed that evening and began dating.

We went steady until three months later when I was shipped out to another base. We became serious and wrote several times a week. After a year we were thinking about the possibility of getting married. Then I received my wings and commission as a second lieutenant. Months went by and, unfortunately for me, she met a nice fellow who already had his commission and wings and was stationed nearby.

I still recall the sorrow when I received her "Dear John" letter that said: "I know this will be somewhat of a shock to you, but mother announced my engagement to Lt. X, last evening."

Life went on, but I kept all of Phyllis' letters and photos. Sixty years later in 2003, I wondered whether Phyllis was even still alive. I wrote to her college and learned she was still with us and it was all right to contact her. I sent her a letter asking if she'd like me to send her letters back. Phyllis replied that she'd like to have the old letters, and brought me up to date on her life.

She'd had a good marriage that was blessed with five children. I also learned, very sadly, that her husband had died of cancer at age 47. After some 10 years, Phyllis married a neighbor whose wife had also passed away. Her second husband, Dick, had recently passed on at about the same time that Sally, my wife of fifty-four years, had died. We started a nice letter communication, ,and I began to consider making the trip to Syracuse, New York, and maybe, just maybe, seeing if she remembered how to play Padiddle.

We never know what is going to happen in life. By circumstance, I was sent to Syracuse. You know I had to make contact, and low and behold, I was pleased to learn Phyllis had not forgotten how to play Padiddle.

Phyllis in 1943   Bill in 1945

Together in 2009. W. S. Hart photos

TRAINS & TROLLEYS

Clang, clang, clang went the trolley

This catchy melody represents the era around 1918 when streetcars were at the height of popularity. Riding rails started with the horse car in the middle 1820s. When electricity came in around 1880, the urban populace was eager for inexpensive and reliable transportation.

After 1918, there was a steady decline in riders as automobile production increased, roads were improved and people wanted the privacy and convenience of their own cars. For all practical purposes, the streetcar passed into oblivion by 1941.

The first self-propelled streetcars received power from an overhead electric wire. A troll or trolley, which was a small wheel, ran on the wire and sent current down a thin pole to the car's motor. The car rested on two sets of four-wheeled trucks. Because each axle had a motor, all eight wheels had pulling power.

The familiar "clang" noise came from a circular metal gong secured under the floorboards near the motorman's stool. A plunger rod extended up through the floor, and the motorman stepped on it to activate a spring-loaded clapper inside the gong.

Trolley routes usually had a hub in the center of a city and extended out to surrounding towns. At the end of the line, the streetcar didn't turn around. The motorman removed the control handle and attached it to a console at the other end of the car. He redistributed the power contact by going outside to what would become the rear of the car. He pulled a rope to lower the trolley pole into contact with that motor. He also raised the pole at the other end to break contact, putting that trolley wheel in the following position.

The seats' backrests had hinged rods at their bases, and for the return trip they were reversed so passengers faced forward. The motorman walked down the aisle, and using both arms, he grabbed the curved handle atop each seat and flipped the seatbacks on both sides of the aisle.

Last, he transferred the metal token box to its new location. The top had four glass sides so you could watch your token go down the chute. When the motorman hit a lever, the coins went through a little door to be stored below. Periodically a small crank was turned on the side of the box to record the fares.

Tokens cost ten cents each or three for a quarter. Fare limits were set according to sections of a route and each section cost one token. You could switch to other routes within your zone with a paper transfer.

School children bought passes at school, and the motorman punched the ticket for each ride. The operator also made change from a shiny, five-inch-tall metal device on his belt. Four cylinders held tokens, nickels, dimes, and quarters. He thumb-punched a lever on the side, and a coin dropped into his hand through a slot in the bottom of the tube.

In winter, the cars' electric heat was adequate and the interior lighting was fine for reading. During morning and evening rush hours most riders had their heads buried in a newspaper. I enjoyed watching the passing scenery or reading the overhead advertising signs that ran the length of the car on both sides. On a crowded car, standees in the center aisle steadied themselves by holding onto leather straps suspended from the ceiling.

Trolleys created a degree of danger in the city. Trolleys ran down the center of the street, and occasionally a passing automobile struck a rider stepping off a streetcar. In large cities there were two sets of tracks. A rider sometimes exited a trolley, walked behind it to cross the street and was hit by a trolley coming from the opposite direction on the second track.

In the 1930s, most communities didn't have good snow removal equipment. Many side streets weren't cleared for days. The streetcar companies had large work cars with tall-bladed plows to clear the tracks and it was common to walk the cleared tracks for local errands.

When I was a kid some of us used to hide and wait for a trolley to stop. We'd jump on and go to the rear of the car. We'd grab the rope that pulled the little wheel from the overhead line; the motor stopped and the lights went out. The motorman came storming out to catch us. I don't recall ever being caught.

Years ago, cities were honeycombed with tracks that connected to faraway places. In New England we rode with ease from New York City to Boston. You could travel from Waterville, Maine to Sheboygan, Wisconsin.

Excursions took people to ballparks, fairgrounds and amusement parks such as Riverside in Massachusetts or Lake Compounce and Savin Rock in Connecticut. People climbed aboard and traveled to the ocean or Long Island Sound just for a shore dinner.

We looked forward to summer and the open-air cars. Rather than entering up front by the operator, you stepped up onto planks that ran the length of the car on both sides and took a seat. Riding those open cars down along the Connecticut River to the shoreline, we all smelled the breeze to catch the first hint of salt air.

My age may show if I talk about riding a trolley with a date, but this quotation from The *Sante Fe Railroad Magazine* says it all:

"Any girl can be gay in a Chevy "Coupaay"

In a taxicab all can be jolly.

But the girl worth the while is the one who can smile

When you're taking her home in a trolley."

"All aboard"

I marvel at anyone who can remember, and keep straight, even a few names of the myriad railroads and the various mergers and failures that occurred during the height of the steam train era from 1900 to the 1940s.

In Connecticut there were several railway companies: The Central New England Railroad and The New York, New Haven, and Hartford were most impressive. By 1902, the Central New England line went from Campbell Hall, New York, near Poughkeepsie, to Hartford, Connecticut. A branch line went northeast from Tariffville to Springfield, Massachusetts.

In 1848, the Canal Railroad built a rail line over much of the old towpath that the discontinued Farmington Canal had used. It ran from New Haven to Northampton, Massachusetts. In 1887, the New York, New Haven and Hartford took over the Canal Railroad operation.

People living in the Granby area in the early 1900s were by no means isolated. Prior to highway systems and motor vehicles, people traveled at a slow pace by a horse and wagon to reach a railroad depot. Once on a train, however, towns whizzed by more quickly than we do today with a modern car.

How great, in those calmer days, to board a passenger car at Granby Station, located on Hartford Avenue in East Granby, and ride north to Congamond Ponds at Southwick, Massachusetts. One could continue

on to shop in Westfield or perhaps have dinner at the Wiggins Tavern in
Northampton.

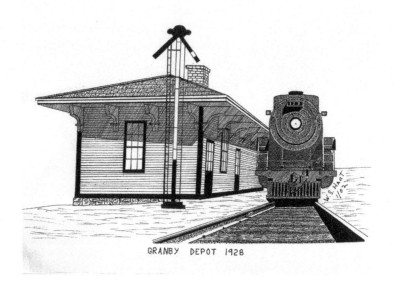

GRANBY DEPOT 1928

The Granby Depot on Hartford Avenue.
Pen and ink drawing by W. S. Hart

Some headed south from Granby station for errands in Simsbury, Avon,
or Farmington. Others visited with relatives in Plainville or Southington or
spent a Saturday in New Haven at the Yale Bowl. The more adventurous
stayed overnight in New York City and enjoyed the entertainment.

Getting from Granby to Hartford was time consuming. It required
driving a wagon to Tariffville, putting the horse in a livery and riding the
train through Bloomfield to Union Station in Hartford.

The attractions of Boston, Massachusetts, were within reach. Once at
Hoskins Station, located across from the present intersection of Route 10
and Hoskins Road in Simsbury, the train proceeded through Tariffville,
East Granby, West Suffield, Feeding Hills, Agawam Junction, Springfield
and on to Boston.

A train ride to a vacation spot in the New York Catskills, or a stay at
Twin Lakes or Salisbury near Canaan, Connecticut, was easily accomplished
by boarding the New York, New Haven and Hartford at Granby for a short
ride to Simsbury, then transferring to the Central New England to head

west for a trip through Tootin' Hills, Canton Village and Collinsville to New Hartford.

Today, in New Hartford—west on Route 44 past Satan's Kingdom and the Waring Manufacturing Company—the houses on the south side of the road still have tin roofs. The tin protected them from the sparks that flew from passing trains as sweating firemen shoveled coal into the fireboxes to feed the flames that kept the boilers at temperatures high enough to maintain a head of steam.

After New Hartford there were stops at Winsted, Norfolk, and Canaan where the antique station stands as a showcase today. Those traveling to the Catskills continued on through Millerton, New York, and crossed the Hudson River on the huge Poughkeepsie railroad bridge that still lives on in all its rusting glory.

Until the demise of the steam locomotives in the 1940s—riding across the country was pleasant and punctual. The passenger cars were clean. Dining car food and the service was a matter of pride. The comfort of sleeping in a Pullman car berth with its crisp white sheets is worth recalling.

In a relaxed mood, it was fun to watch the panoply of towns, farms, woods and houses go by. Railcars stopped and waited at the occasional railroad crossing where red lights flashed and the warning signal's "clang-ang-ang-angs" seemed muted.

My nostalgia recalls the eerie sounds of the long and short blasts of the engine's whistle at the crossings, the toll of its bell at depots, and the "woof, woof-woof" sound from the smokestack as the iron horse labored to get moving and the wheels spun for traction on the shiny rails.

Stop, look and listen!

Most men from my generation have fond memories of their fascination with steam trains prior to World War II. For me, driving past the 1853 Granby railroad station brings a flood of memories.

When I was in grade school in the 1930s, the impact of Hartford's Union Station on local and long distance travel was tremendous. It was a travel hub long before the era of airports with their jumbo jets flying off in all directions.

On occasion my father was sent by his company to visit district offices in Pennsylvania. He took a "sleeper" out of Hartford on Sunday nights. He slept in an upper or lower berth on a Pullman car and ate in the dining car.

The first time I was taken to the depot as a child, my mother led me by the hand because I was so busy looking at everything. On the upper platform I heard the approaching train somewhere out in the darkness. The massive black, snorting engine with its lone Cyclops headlight slowly bore down on the waiting people and made the planked platform tremble under my feet. It puffed heavy smoke. Its bell clanged. Steam spewed out from under it and from between the cars. Looking up at those huge wood-spoked iron wheels almost took my breath away.

The expansive and high-ceilinged lower level was the waiting room. It was furnished with rows of long solid-wood benches placed back to back. Every sound became a great echo that reverberated throughout the room, especially the information booth's speaker system that blared out arrivals and departures. The clear tones of the announcer called out the train name or number, the track number, the time it was arriving or departing and what cities it was coming from or going to.

There was a fine small restaurant plus a sparkling gift shop where a traveler could buy a memento. Traveling men stepped up onto a two-tiered marble structure, sat in a chair and placed their feet on a brass support for a first-class shoeshine. Sometimes a skilled "bootblack" showed off with a snapping-quick rhythm of his polishing cloth when he finished his task. Outside the east entrance, buses and taxis waited to serve the passengers.

When my father departed, a redcap handed his valise to a porter on the train; the conductor stood by with a low stool and helped people ascend to the higher steps on the car.

While the passengers boarded, the engineer, in a gray cloth cap with a blue lining, moved around the hissing engine with a long-necked oil can lubricating the various junction boxes and bearings, and did a visual safety inspection of his iron horse.

When all was set, the conductor checked a big pocket watch that hung from his vest pocket by a long chain, and hollered, "All board." Shortly, the engineer pulled the throttle lever, and the sweating fireman shoveled coal into the flaming firebox.

In an instant, the mammoth wheels took the surge of steam and spun on the shiny tracks until the engineer backed off the power to let the wheels get a grip. Slowly, the mammoth wheels turned as the long pitman arms drove them forward. One last wave from my father, and he was off to Pittsburgh.

Presently, dikes protect Hartford from the Connecticut River, and the Park River runs underground through Bushnell Park. In the 1930s most every spring, low sections of Hartford flooded. The Hartford *Times* and the *Courant* ran pictures of a passenger stepping into a rowboat at the train station and another of this person, still in the boat, signing the register at the desk in the lobby of the Bond Hotel just up Asylum Street.

During World War II, between 1942 and 1945, I rode many troop trains. We rode in coach cars sitting in groups of four in double seats that faced each other. To sleep, we scrunched down and rested our feet beside the guy across the way. The repetitive clickety-clack, clickety-clack lulled you into a sleep of sorts. However, you frequently woke with a crick in your neck from the train's constant lurching.

I recall pulling into Grand Central Station in New York City where we stopped next to an aluminum-sided Streamliner. The people on board that train wore nice street clothes and were being served dinner by white coated waiters. We all had a two-day growth of beard, were sleepy-eyed and covered with engine soot and grime. On our train meals were served as we filed through a boxcar holding a paper plate—not even tin. Most meals consisted of a bologna sandwich on stale bread, a green apple and lukewarm coffee. Seeing the fancy streamliner next to us, we couldn't help but think that something was wrong with the system.

What has stayed in my memory of all those train rides and stations is that, in those days, toilets emptied directly onto the tracks as the train rolled along. As we pulled into a platform, it became common for the whole car of soldiers to sing "passengers will please refrain from flushing toilets while the train is standing at the station platform"—sung to the melody of Humoresque by Dvorak.

A LIFELONG LOVE AFFAIR WITH CARS

How times have changed

I learned to drive a car in 1937 when I was fourteen years old. In my teens, I spent summers at my grandfather's farm in North Granby. The depression was in full swing and Uncle Beach and his family survived by living from what the farm produced.

Apparently my uncle considered me the son he never had and we got along famously. He had very little money, so I worked for room and board. The only cash I had was the dollar a week my father sent to me.

Seven days a week we milked, by hand, twenty head of cows morning and night. In between we tended the chickens, a truck garden and harvested the crops.

That summer, Uncle Beach decided I should learn to drive so I could do chores that required using the farm vehicles. One corn lot had just been cut off, and it was clear except for rows of six-inch cornstalk stubs. Uncle Beach drove us over there in the 1928 Whippet sedan. He left the motor running, got out. He said, "Go to it" and walked back to the house.

I'd seen people driving—shifting gears and pushing pedals—but that was all I knew. I did some things with the clutch, and stalled the car several times before I mastered shifting gears and moving backwards and forward. I steered in clumsy circles and learned how to use the brakes.

The next year, when I was fifteen, I drove pretty good and imagined myself to be old Barney Oldfield, the racecar driver. I zipped around the sixty-five acre farm at a pretty good clip.

One time I smelled smoke from a small fire under the dashboard. I drove the car into the brook and drowned the fire. Another day, I was at the upper hay field and saw my uncle working down on the flats. I figured I could angle down and across the hill and get to him without driving back by the barns and down the dirt road. I inched along until my thick brain told me I couldn't continue without the car tipping over to the left and rolling end-over-end down the hill.

The car was in such a precarious position that I couldn't go forward, and the wheels spun when I tried to back up. I walked down the hill to my uncle and sheepishly told him what I'd done. I give him great credit for his patience. Over the years I'd done some foolish things and broken some equipment, but he never once raised his voice or even criticized me. I'm sure this last stunt tested his will.

He walked back with me and surveyed the situation. He decided to use a twelve-foot fence rail as a lever. He rolled the rear door windows down and shoved the rail through the openings. With the one end of the rail against the top of the far window frame, the other end rested against the window sill of the near door. He grabbed the rail and put pressure on it and had me back up slowly. The leverage gave the rear wheels some traction and we slowly inched the car back up the hill. I recall how guilty I felt. I would have preferred he bawled me out instead of being silent.

When I was sixteen and in high school, my father wouldn't allow me get a driver's license. He said: "I didn't buy that car for you to run around in." Some six months later, the local florist offered me a job driving his delivery truck. I blackmailed my father into giving his approval, but he refused to give me two dollars for the license.

The following Saturday, I rang the neighbors' doorbells and asked if I could wash their windows. I worked all day and earned two dollars; labor was twenty-five cents an hour in those days.

I drove the delivery truck all through high school. My starting pay was twenty-five cents an hour, and I worked my way up to fifty cents. I worked after school and a full day on Saturdays. I put in twenty-three hours and made $5.75 a week. I was independent.

I graduated from high school in 1941, and when Pearl Harbor was struck, I enlisted in the U.S. Army Air Corps. Waiting to be called to service, I worked for a big insurance company as a clerk and earned eighteen-fifty a week. I gave my widowed mother eight dollars for room and board. With the rest, I bought a car for $75 and dated the young ladies. My average paycheck was $88.80 a month—$1,055.60 a year.

I still look upon that era as the "good old days." How times have changed.

My little car

This morning I was grocery shopping in the local chain store that I've used for forty-seven years. The building is old and the aisles very narrow.

As I pushed my cart around one of the corners, it collided with a young child seated in a contraption that looks like a miniature car with a small steering wheel: the back third is a grocery cart. Later, I thought about that little guy, and it took me back to 1925 when I was three years old and we lived in South Orange, New Jersey. I had a little car with a steering wheel that I propelled with two small foot pedals. That metal replica even had a small radiator and grill copied from a 1920s Buick.

My love affair with cars started with this replica of a
1920s Buick. W. S. Hart photo

In my musings, I thought of all of the cars my family owned through the years: a 1925 Studebaker, a 1927 Buick, a 1928 Whippet, a 1928 LaSalle, and the first modern car, a 1934 Buick sedan.

In 1941, when I turned nineteen, I bought my first car—a 1934 Ford roadster for which I paid $75. It was black with yellow spoke wheels and an almost-white convertible top. The seats were real leather. The small rumble seat held two people who entered it by placing their left foot on a small circular step on the rear bumper and stepping up to another small step on the fender with their right foot, which allowed them to easily enter the rumble seat with their left foot. I had one problem with that old car. There was a kink in the gasket on the oil pan. Every time I stopped for a period of time, it left a puddle of oil on the ground. I solved that by carrying an empty coffee can, and each time I stopped I put the can under the leak. Before I took off, I poured the oil back into the crankcase.

I think of my teenage grandchildren hopping into a car with an automatic transmission, power steering, anti-lock brakes, anti-skid control, heater, air-conditioning, cruise control, a ten-speaker audio system and a computer to tell them where they are. My little 1934 roadster had none of those amenities.

Car radios were something you attached under the dashboard and strung wires under the running boards for reception, unlike the fish pole antennas of the 1940s. I couldn't afford a radio, so I had no music. I had no defroster or heater. The car had side curtains rather than roll-up windows, and the wind blew constantly on my left shoulder. Hydraulic brakes hadn't been invented, and old brake shoes constantly went out of adjustment. You never knew in which direction the car would skid if you made a quick stop.

When I lift up the hood of my present car, the engine appears to be completely enclosed with no spark plugs showing, no carburetor, generator, fuel pump, water pump, distributor or, surprisingly, no dip stick to check the oil level. I access the computer with push buttons on the steering wheel to determine whether I need oil. It always amuses me to see the lighted message "check engine," which indicates there is a problem. I obediently open up the hood and, yes, the engine is still there but that's all I know. I appreciate modern cars, but I'm sure other ancient fools like me miss maintaining their own cars.

I still reminisce about that little toy car. I've always loved to drive, and even at the age of three, I'd lie in bed and pretend to drive. I had a spring-activated pistol that shot missiles with rubber suction cups on the end at a circular metal bull's eye target. I propped the target on my knees as a steering wheel and lay there in the dark, making motor sounds and pretending I was driving. When I was perhaps twelve years old, I went out to the garage and sat behind the wheel of the family car, a 1928 LaSalle, and pretended I was racing in the Memorial Day Indianapolis 500.

I've been a car nut all of my life.

Every dog has his day

I think for most men, cars have been a big part of their lives. When I was young and single, I cherished every car I owned. Old paint finishes made keeping a car shiny a constant battle. Three of the most popular cleaners and waxes were Simonize, Turtle Wax and Dupont 7. The car's body surface was cleaned, waxed and polished. It was done with elbow grease: just your arms and hands, no power buffers. I spent hours polishing chrome, cleaning spoke wheels and painting white walls on old black tires.

My cars had wire curb feelers at the bottoms of the front fenders to protect against knocking the wheels out of alignment. I dolled my car up with mud flaps and a spotlight on the driver's doorpost. One car had a fender guide mounted on the top of the right fender. It was a twelve-inch chromium staff with a small light that helped me judge how close I was to another car. About the only thing I didn't have was ball fringe around the rear window. Of course I did have a small plastic dog with a nodding head that sat on the dashboard.

Most kids today won't know what I mean, but I had a necker's knob on the steering wheel. It was like a small doorknob that you used to rotate the wheel. It freed your right arm to put around your date. With no seat belts to separate you, it made for a pleasant drive.

On Decoration Day, which was changed to Memorial Day, we attached a small fan of American flags to the radiator cap and wove red, white and blue tissue paper through the wheel spokes. I added a couple of finishing touches. I attached a foxtail to the antenna and installed a metal plunger through the floorboards that activated the Bermuda bell I mounted underneath. It responded with a two-tone "bong-bong."

I had a V-8 convertible, and I replaced the single muffler with dual mufflers; the motor sounded like a Chris-Craft speedboat with its deep-throated purr. Looking back, I think I understand why my parents had some concerns about where their son was headed. I thought it would be fun to be a car salesman. A local dealer sent me to the General Motors sales school in Tarrytown, New York. They gave us pointers so we could try to live up to the old saying, "You can't beat a man at his own game."

Back in the showroom, I tried to put this knowledge to work. With a couple, I had to determine who ruled the roost and put my efforts in that direction. The first step was noticing the colors the woman was wearing and directing them to cars in that color range. You opened the door to let the woman see the upholstery. If, right away, you discerned that she had no interest, you turned to the man. If he appeared to be a serious type, you talked about the mechanical aspects of the car. If he was a sporty dresser, you steered him to a convertible or a station wagon and emphasized the chrome, the whitewall tires or the quality of the radio.

A pipe smoker was the most difficult customer. To make a sale, in any endeavor, you get the prospect to agree with you—to nod his head in agreement with what you're saying. If you take him down this road far enough, it becomes difficult for him to shake his head no. It was difficult to get this routine going with the pipe smoker. Just as I asked for some agreement, he'd get out his Zippo, tamp the tobacco down and play with lighting that stupid pipe.

The cadence was also broken when a customer broke into my pitch with a technical question so deep that I couldn't answer without walking away to look for the answer.

I starved myself out of the car game and became an insurance adjuster. Dealing with people can be enjoyable but there may be stumbling blocks along the way. Two groups of people that I found hard to deal with were teachers and doctors.

People in these professions are used to having people do as they say. The teacher tells you what homework to do, when to recite, when to go to the blackboard. And when you were in grade school, told you to clean the blackboard and take the erasers outside and clap them. The doctor lives in the same world. He tells you to take off your clothes, what medicines to take, what diet to follow and when to come back for an appointment. I never said no to either one. Having people respond to them in a positive manner is their way of life. They had a tough time accepting that I wouldn't pay the amount they anticipated or, worse still, that their claim wasn't covered.

It's so pleasant to be retired and out of the rat race. If you're not there yet, remember, "All good things come to him who waits." Some day it'll be your turn because—every dog has his day.

Running boards and rumble seats

Prior to 1940 most cars had running boards. A popular model was the roadster with a rumble seat. I have never learned why the boards were "running" and the seats "rumble." Maybe some of you over-the-hill people, like me, have some fun memories of rumble seats.

To open the seat, you stood by the right rear of the car, rested your left foot on a small metal step on top of the bumper and swung your right foot to a step atop the fender. From this perch, you leaned over, turned a door handle and pulled up the seat lid.

Double dating on a moonlit summer night was pleasant as you could sit back there in real privacy. You were forced to sit close together, and the couple up front couldn't hear your private conversation.

I most admired the rumble seat in the Model A Ford. The engine had four cylinders with very low RPM. The almost musical sound from a well-tuned engine came out of the exhaust pipe just below the rear bumper—and the rumble seat.

1930 Model A Ford Roadster.
Photo by Happy Days Dream Cars at: www.happycarz.com

The seats in cars built before 1940 were higher from the ground than today's sedans, so the running board was a convenient way to step into the car. On larger sedans, running boards were helpful when you packed the car for a vacation or trip. Luggage of various sizes could be stored there and held in place by a scissors-like expanding black metal gate. For additional storage, most cars had a folding rack attached to the back of the car capable of carrying a steamer trunk.

If you wanted to be spiffy in the 20s and 30s, you put fresh flowers in the two glass vases mounted on the inner doorposts.

I recall that in 1942 when I was waiting to go into WWII, my friend Gil had a 1932 Buick convertible with a rumble seat. We were still a little wild and did stupid things. One day four of us piled into the old car with a specific purpose in mind. We drove to Tunxis Avenue in Bloomfield where the two-lane blacktop highway was straight for a few miles. Gil and I were up front with the canvas top down. We had cut two pieces of clothesline and tied one to the left spoke of the steering wheel and the other to the right spoke.

A lever on the wheel let you set the throttle to any constant speed desired. We set it at 30 MPH before Gil opened his door and stood on the running board. I did the same on my side. Each holding a piece of clothesline, we climbed over the rear fenders and stood on the back bumper, happily steering down the highway with our two pals sitting in the rumble seat with their arms crossed like two coachmen.

Can you imagine what oncoming drivers must have thought when they saw that car coming at them with nobody in the driver's seat? When a curve came up, we quickly retraced our paths to the front seat.

If I'm not mistaken there was an old song with the words, "Rah, rah, rumble seats and running boards: Them was the good old days."

The black and white movies of the 1930s portrayed college kids running around in old open cars. They wore raccoon coats, saddle shoes and porkpie hats and they looked terribly young. They sang oldies such as "Happy Days are Here Again" or "Flat Foot Floogie."

My favorite jukebox tune was: "No, No, They Can't Take That Away From Me."

My new car is smarter than I

I just took delivery on a new car that is computerized and digitally expressive. After a drive-around-the-block familiarization ride, I cautiously drove the twelve miles home through highway traffic.

The manufacturer fully realized that an old fool like me needs more instruction. The owner's packet has a DVD to walk me through each gadget's operation. To make sure I understand, there's also a CD that re-emphasizes, step-by-step, what to do.

Twixt thee and me, I have no interest in an electric key to open doors, turn on lights and open the trunk. I'm sure I don't need heated and remotely controlled outside mirrors. I don't really need to know the outside or inside temperatures. It's gilding the lily to have a chime alert me that some road surfaces may be slippery with black ice. Since 1938, I have driven thousands of miles without an anti-lock brake system that is supposed to prevent me from skidding.

The in-car computer tells me when I need an oil change, when a door isn't shut or the emergency brake is on. At any given instant I can check how many miles per gallon I'm getting and how far I can drive before filling up. It even computes my average miles-per-hour. While all this nonsense is going on, I am soothed by music from the ten camouflaged stereo speakers.

I can't begin to recount the available options that weren't standard equipment on my car. All I know is that I didn't need any of them.

Many Miles Ago

A couple of weeks past I took a solitary trip to Maine in a car I bought in 2000. I traveled a super highway and set the cruise control at 70 MPH. These new cars have no wind noise, the engines are quiet and road sounds are muffled.

The car has ten speakers that create a circle of music. I played a favorite CD from "The Music Man," a classic movie that starred Robert Preston. The first song is from a scene on a passenger train where a group of traveling salesmen are conversing. I thought about the changes in transportation that allowed those hucksters to sell their wares more easily. The 1933 Ford I used in sales back in 1948 popped into my thoughts.

I was single and earning about $2,400 a year. I found the car in a run-down repair garage in the North End of Hartford. It was exposed to the elements and piled high with old tires, car parts and dead batteries.

On the spur of the moment, I told the garage guy I'd give him $100 if he could get it running. He told me to come back the next day, and even though the car still looked dilapidated, the old thing sat there idling and ready to go.

A 1933 Ford Phaeton in a similar state to the one I purchased in Hartford.
Photo by Dick Shappy at: www.classiccars.com

After a few days of work, I got the electrics working and it passed state inspection. The inspector laughed when he saw the car, and was surprised when he found the vehicle mechanically sound. Remember, that old bucket of bolts was 15 years old.

It was a Phaeton, which meant it had a convertible canvass top and four doors. The leather seats cleaned up just fine with saddle soap and I sewed up a tear in the canvass. I steam cleaned the engine and used Dupont 7 to give the black body and fenders a beautiful shine.

I removed the wire wheels and painted the spokes cherry red. After cleaning the sides of the tires, I painted them with a rubberized paint, which turned them into eye-catching white walls. After the chrome grill, bumpers and hubcaps got a good polishing, the old car looked pretty good.

Unlike modern cars, Phaetons had "suicide doors" that hinged near the shoulders of the front seats and opened at the dashboard junctures. If a door popped open while you were driving, it slammed back against the side of the car.

It had no heater, defroster or radio. My car was originally fitted with side curtains but they were missing, and with cold air also rushing in through the cracks in the floorboards, it's difficult to describe how cold it was in frigid weather. When it rained, I got soaked.

At the time I was courting my wife, Sally, who lived in Farmington. One Sunday night we went to Cherry Park Stadium in Canton. This was prior to the Canton/Avon town line being moved. If the track existed today, it would be in Avon.

The park had a dirt oval track where midget cars raced every Sunday night. After the races we walked around the pit area under the glare of overhead lights. The drivers, Bill Schindler, Johnny Rice, Ted Tappet, Eddie Flernke and King Carpenter stood by their Offenhausers and talked with fans. The car's exhaust pipes were still hot, and the engine blocks made cracking and snapping sounds as they cooled down.

Sally and I headed home and drove down Waterville Road or Route 10. In 1948 there was little traffic after ten o'clock in that rural area. There was no moon and, at that moment, no cars driving towards us or following us. The ragtop was down and the wind whipped our hair and made the tips of our cigarettes glow as we relived the races.

Suddenly, I was driving blind! Without a hint of trouble, impenetrable darkness! With a clutching stomach and breath held, my mind whirled. Blind? No! The headlights were out. "Come on jerk, think," don't lock the breaks, steer straight, but drift slightly to the left until you feel the gravel shoulder of the road and stop slowly.

Breathless, and still full of panic, I realized a fuse had blown. There were no spare fuses in the glove compartment. As I had done before, I ripped open my pack of Chesterfields, removed the tinfoil and wrapped it around the old fuse. The lights responded instantly, and we continued on to her home.

During our courtship we often returned to her parents' place and sat in the parlor until all hours. The rusted muffler on the ancient Ford was loud. To avoid disturbing her parents or the neighbors when I left, I pushed the car down the road to a grade, jumped in, put it in gear and let out the clutch, which started the engine. That's when I turned on the headlights and drove contentedly, though noisily, into the night.

How dumb can I get?

I wonder how many of you feel as dumb as I do when you attempt to master today's wonderful mechanical and electronic gadgets? I find myself using expressive World War II expletives when I try to program the VCR.

I keep the nearby window locked so I won't be tempted to throw my computer out of it. When I'm halfway through writing a page and the paragraph shifts, or I lose the screen entirely, I again use those folksy service words.

My self-starting snow blower and sit-down lawn mower are kept running by a John Deere dealer that also looks after the brush cutter and the weed whacker.

My 2004 car is completely computerized. I frequently drive to the dealership to have them explain or set something for me. Its memory system stows the whims of three different drivers. A button allows me to set the seat, steering wheel and outside mirrors to my specifications. When I insert my key, each little motor does its thing and the various units snap to attention and adjust everything to my preferences.

I push a key button when I approach the car, and the headlights come on and the doors unlock. If the car is parked in a big dark parking lot, I can push another button, and a warning device tells me just where the car is located. If I have packages, still another button opens the trunk.

When I leave the car in the yard at night, a light on the bottom of the door lights up the ground so I won't fall on my face. The headlights remain on until I get to the kitchen door. Unfortunately, I still have to dig the house key out of my pocket and physically turn it in the lock myself.

In the morning when I back out of the driveway, the right outside mirror tilts down so I can see where my rear wheel is—as if I didn't know. I can't forget to hook my seat belt because a gismo comes forward over my left shoulder and presents the end of the belt; no more groping behind the seat with my left hand. I finally located the hood latch, and after using it, discovered the engine is all enclosed. I can't see a carburetor, spark plugs, air filter, generator, fan or distributor.

The only service I can safely perform on my car is to wash it. I won't even try to change a tire. Only a mechanical engineer can get the jack out of the trunk and raise the car. Even if I stumbled onto the proper way to put the spare on, it must be torqued to a specified foot-poundage.

Way back when, I had a rebuilt motor installed in a car I owned at the time. Before it was put in, I cleaned the firewall and painted it black. When the engine arrived, I painted it marine gray and all the attachments either red or shiny black. It was fun to open the hood to show off that spotless engine compartment to one of my buddies.

I couldn't afford whitewall tires so I bought rubberized paint and did the tires myself. After a while the white turned yellow and job had to be repeated.

It is unheard of today, but back in the 1940s I hand-painted my car with a three-inch brush and Ducco lacquer. There were a few brush marks that I smoothed out with a slightly abrasive rubbing compound. Simonize Car Wax and a lot of elbow grease completed the job. No electric buffer for me. The old car looked showroom new.

I appreciate today's heaters, defrosters, air conditioners, radios, headlights, tinted glass and anti-lock brakes, but I miss the simple pleasures of working on my own car.

You're never too old

A while back I was sitting by the Farmington River near the old Hitchcock Chair Factory in Riverton. I saw and heard the call of a nearby red-winged blackbird, which cut into the soft flowing sounds of the river. People look for quiet moments like this, and in that quiet, I drifted back in thought to when this little community was a busy place.

Suddenly, I heard a loud, poorly muffled motorcycle screeching down the road. The bearded rider wore a bandanna instead of a helmet, and his sleeveless shirt exaggerated his multi-tattooed arms. I was reminded of the old saying, "You can tell a happy motorcyclist by counting the bugs in his teeth."

I don't condemn this guy; everyone has the right to walk to the beat that pleases him. Furthermore, I'm not putting him down because, at age eighty-three, I still ride a motorcycle. A red, 250cc Honda Rebel that's great for cruising country roads in our beautiful New England.

Until 2000, I exclusively rode a dirt bike through the challenging woodlands in our area. I started riding at age fifty-three when most sensible people have given up this dangerous sport.

My son, Will, was involved in motocross racing in Southwick, Massachusetts, and at other courses. He practiced in the sand pits near where we live. I was watching him one day and he said, "Dad, give it a try." I said "no way." He replied, "You can ride a bicycle can't you?" I got on and he showed me low gear, how to let out the clutch and give it the gas. I tooled around for quite a while and gradually learned how to shift gears and use the brakes.

I was hooked. I bought a used dirt bike with big, knobby tires. In the past thirty years, I've had seven bikes and only the current one is a street bike.

Outfitted for the trail. W. S. Hart photo

Dirt bikes are not legal on the highways, so I bought a two-rail trailer. I hauled my cycle to East Hartland and other trail areas, parked off the road and took off into the woods. I rode every Saturday and Sunday from March until December, and put on fifty to sixty miles each time I went out. I bought topographical maps of the area and laid out routes over old logging roads, power lines, trails and swamps.

There is great risk in riding a dirt bike alone, but I couldn't find any other old fool to go with me, but I was determined to ride. I drew all of my routes on the maps and numbered each one. I always left a list of route numbers with my wife so that if I didn't come home for supper, a rescue crew would know where to look for my old bones.

Street bike riding, to me, is really for sissies. You sit there and go straight and level on a smooth pavement with no challenges at all. On a dirt bike you ride standing up, and work the rough trails using your thigh muscles in the same way a skier does. Riding up and down rocky terrain and across streams you have to balance the bike under you.

On a scale of one to ten, I rate a street bike as about a four while I consider a dirt bike a ten. Most everyone can ride the easy highways, but not all can stand up to the rugged workout of trail riding.

In a standing position, your left hand grips the handlebar and two fingers work the clutch lever. The right hand turns the throttle on or off, and two fingers work the front brake lever. While working through tough areas, your left foot moves the shift lever up and down, and the right foot controls the rear brake. You coordinate all of these actions while maintaining your balance.

You might ride a street bike at 50 or 60 mph but on a dirt bike in the woods the going is slower. If you go down it isn't so horrendous. There are, however, real hazards. Over the years I have "looped it," which means the front wheel comes up off the ground fast and you go over backwards with a chance the bike will land on top of you. An "endo" is when the front wheel digs in and the rear wheel, along with you, goes over it and again, the bike may nail you.

If you ride across a steep side hill, and you fall toward the upper slope, it's called "going off the low side." If you fall off the bike down the slope, it's "going off the high side." Both actions grab your attention in a hurry.

When a person first starts dirt biking he usually gets into trouble in a panic situation. At the instant of trouble your hands and feet freeze and, as a result, you don't back off the gas, hit the brakes or pop the clutch. I've mowed down a lot of brush in those situations.

To solve the panic problem, I did a practice run each time I rode. Traveling at 30 mph, I'd think "crash" and after a while it became second nature to hit the brakes, pop the clutch and skid to a stop. While balanced there, I downshifted to first gear without touching the ground and took off again. This saved me many a time in the woods.

To protect my aging body, I always wore Full Bore boots that came up to my knees. I had knee and elbow pads, a leather jacket, helmet, goggles, a mouth guard and heavy riding pants.

My biggest surprise occurred in West Granville when I was riding a familiar logging road. Since my previous ride, beavers had built a dam downstream that flooded the area I rode. I was on the pegs riding in a foot or so of muddy water at a reasonable speed when suddenly, with no hint of trouble, I hit a submerged rock. The bike flipped to the right, and I did a somersault over the bars and rolled to a sitting position in two feet of water. It was an eerie and confusing feeling when I sat up with my goggles half filled with water, and as I watched, the level gradually receded as the water leaked out of the vents.

In a stunned condition, I sat there for a while looking at one handle bar sticking out of the water. I finally got to my feet and pushed the bike to dry ground. I emptied the water out of my boots, and silently looked up to the skies and gave thanks I hadn't been busted up in the flip.

When a bike goes under water, the running motor sucks water through the air filter into the carburetor and the engine quits. If you try to kick-start a wet motor you can explode the cylinder, so you follow a procedure. The bike is turned upside down to rest on the handlebars. The air filter is removed and the water squeezed out. The spark plug is removed, and finally you kick the motor over by hand to force the water out of the piston.

I did all the right things, turned the bike upright and it started with the first kick. Success!

My happy spirits were soon dashed. I got on, put it in gear and gave it the gas: It quit. I was ten miles into the woods, and I started to get a little worried. I decided to turn the idle screw up, which revved the motor a little higher. It still wouldn't go with me on the bike. I tried walking beside it in first gear, but it stalled at the smallest grade. My sluggish brain finally figured out that there was water in the gasoline bowl. I carefully loosened the bottom screw, drained the water out and everything was all right.

As I rode the many miles out, I was pleased that I had dodged another bullet. The old fool was still riding and nobody had come looking for me.

Still riding in my 80s! W. S. Hart photo

When I turned seventy-eight in the year 2000, I got it though my head that I shouldn't be out there riding alone. I stepped down to my present street bike. I still see no challenge to street riding, but at least I feel the wind on my face, feel the bike respond to my control, and smile when I "count the bugs in my teeth." See? You're never too old.

For men only

I can't think of any women who will have any interest in what I'm about to write. Come to think of it, I don't imagine any guy under age fifty will relate to this either.

I was thumbing through an old photo album compiled between 1936 and 1950, and noted several pictures of cars I used to own. There's a wide spread of change from those early models to the electronic marvels of today.

I began to think of car things that have come and gone. I began jotting them down and it became quite a list. Do you aging car buffs recall any of the following that relate to some vehicle you owned back when?

Radiator caps with a built-in thermometer, striping brushes, engine cranks, curb feelers, fender guides, fancy gear shift, steering wheel "necking" knob, leaky floor boards, transverse springs, "knee-action" suspension, golf club compartment door, fox tails, painted on white walls, mud flaps, lap robes, hot air manifold heaters, gasoline heaters, radios hung under the dash, antennas under the running board, ball fringe tacked around the windows, Bermuda bell, Ah-ooga horns, "cut-out" slide on the manifold to make sound bypass the muffler, dual exhausts for a "Chris-Craft" sound, eyelids on the headlights in case of an air raid, musical horns, snap-on grill covers, tire chains with rubber spreaders to maintain tension, monkey links to repair a broken cross chain, the first mud tires that later proved great as snow tires, re-grooved tires, recapped tires with tubes, tube patching kits, blow-out patches, mechanical brakes adjusted at each wheel by a wrench and turnbuckles on the brake rods, checking toe-in with a string, putting rocks in the trunk for winter ballast, when the gearshift moved from the floor to the steering wheel, heated-wire glass defroster with suction cups, rubber-bladed fans to clear steam from the back or front windows, glass windscreens on each side of the windshield, canvass tonneau covers, spare tire covers, chains with quiet rubber links, plate glass windows, free-wheeling, metal visors that shaded the top of the windshield, plastic half-moon stuck to the bottom of the windshield to reflect overhead traffic lights that the visor hid, roadster side curtains with a hole by the elbow so you stick your arm out for hand signals, purple-dot taillights, cigarette lighters on a retractable electric cord, two glass flower vases on the inside door posts, one-piece windshields that cranked up for ventilation, how wet it could get in a rumble seat, real leather seats, seat covers, jump seats, foot rests, spotlights, bumper mounted fog or back-up lights, fender skirts, chrome exhaust extensions, scissors or bumper jacks, undercoating, gas rationing sticker on the windshield, metal license plate inserts to prove registration, hand-applied cleaners and waxes such as Simonize or Blue Coral, Dupont 7 liquid auto polish, trunk rack, expanding luggage gate on a running board, a roll down curtain on the rear window before non-glare mirrors, chrome license frames, colored glass reflector buttons, dash mounted compass.

Today, if something goes wrong, an idiot light tells me "check engine." Years ago we took care of minor repairs with a set of open end or socket wrenches, a pair of pliers, some screw drivers and a hammer. We relined brakes, changed the points, gapped the plugs and replaced the coil, condenser and hoses or belts.

It just ain't fun no more.

GRANBY'S NOTABLE CITIZENS

The Revolution—Captain Hays' Company

Walk through older sections of some Granby burial grounds, and you'll find commemorative markers that identify the graves of soldiers who fought in the American Revolution. Several headstones also mention that the man beneath the marker served in Captain Samuel Hays' Company.

Those headstones had little meaning for me until recently when I went through a trunk of old papers left by a long-deceased veteran. One of note was a printed application for membership in the Sons of the American Revolution (SAR), which is the brother organization to the Daughters of the American Revolution (DAR).

The application showed this person was claiming his right to be a member because he was related to Moses Gossard, a soldier of the Revolutionary War who is buried in the West Granby cemetery. Attached to the application was a hand-written letter from the office of the Adjutant General's Office, State of Connecticut at Hartford, dated February 7, 1898.

Of special interest were Moses Gossard's dates of service: August 22, 1776, to September 25, 1776, about one month. According to the letter, he served as a Private in Captain Hays' Company of the 18th Regiment under Colonel Jonathan Pettibone of Simsbury.

The startling part of the letter was the statement that these troops contributed to the battle often referred to as the Panic at Kip's Bay. Digging further into the facts behind that statement was difficult because old military records from 1776 were not clearly defined or properly preserved.

A book compiled in 1889 by the Authority of the General Assembly in Hartford, lists a somewhat complete history of the records of Service for Connecticut men during the Revolution.

In 1776 there were three types of military service:

- Continental Troops constituted the body of George Washington's Army in the field throughout the war. In 1776 Connecticut raised eight Regiments.
- State Troops were neither Continental nor Militia, but were raised as necessary as reinforcements to the army in the field.
- Militia was the third distinctive class of troop, and was the standing Militia in the state. The Militia represented the greater part of the male population. The number of effective Militia during the war years ranged from 22,000 to 25,000 men.

One of the triggers for the panic at Kip's Bay occurred on Saint Patrick's Day in 1776 when, under pressure from General George Washington's troops, the British commander, Sir William Howe, gave up the siege of Boston and evacuated the city. Washington felt certain Howe would join his brother, Admiral Lord Howe, the commander of the British Fleet and proceed to take New York City.

To assist his limited Continental Troops, General Washington requested that Connecticut send him a portion of its Militia. Connecticut already had nine state and eight Continental Regiments on active duty. Connecticut put out two requisitions. The first for fourteen Regiments of Militia from west of the Connecticut River to serve from August "until the Exigency should be over." The second was for nine Regiments east of the river to serve from September on.

Captain Samuel Hays' Company was summoned to active duty from Granby, which was then Salmon Brook Society and part of ancient Simsbury. Records show the unit consisted of twenty-five enlisted men and three officers. Most were Holcombs and four were Gossards. Tilly Gossard, age thirty, was listed as drummer.

Captain Hays' company marched to New Haven and boarded a boat that landed them at Flatbush on Long Island on August 22, 1776. The company became part of the 18th Regiment led by Colonel Jonathan Pettibone. Shortly thereafter, on August 27, 1776, American troops lost the Battle of Long Island, and the military powers gave much thought to evacuating New York City. General Washington decided not to withdraw from the entire island, but divided his men between Manhattan and the mainland at Kingsbridge.

The British, under Admiral Howe, sent gunboats and troopships up the East River hoping to isolate the island of Manhattan. On September 12 the Americans moved out but they still had troops on the lower island. Suddenly, on Sunday morning, September 15, 1776, the British forces struck at Kip's Bay, which was located about where 34th street and the East River are today.

A Connecticut Brigade under Colonel William Douglas failed to hold its position. The "scarlet-laden boats looking like a large clover field in full bloom" landed on Manhattan with little resistance.

General Washington, only four miles away in Harlem, rushed to the scene. The panic he observed infuriated him. The supporting brigades of Colonel Samuel Parsons of Connecticut and General Fellows of Massachusetts were in wild retreat. Washington and Putnam used every means in their power to rally the troops, but to no avail. The "distasteful and dastardly conduct of the troops," as Washington described it, compelled him to withdraw toward Harlem, though not before he came perilously close to being captured.

With morale at a low point, many of the poorly disciplined troops deserted. An estimated 6,000 out of 8,000 Connecticut Militiamen deserted. Colonel John Mead's Regiment from the Stamford area dwindled from six hundred to seventy four men.

Colonel Gold S. Silliman said: "for as well the officers and the men belonging to the Militia, behaved extremely ill; and officers of all ranks & privates kept deserting & running off, in a most shameful scandalous manner; and some were taken sick and a great many more pretended to be so."

Washington wrote to his brother, Augustine: "The game is pretty near up." He placed the blame chiefly on the "accursed policy of short enlistments" and "too great a dependence on the militia."

The 1889 volume, "Record of Service of Connecticut Man," treated the troops more kindly by saying, "as these troops were hastily summoned, poorly trained and provided for, and generally undisciplined, effective service could not be expected of them.

"Better troops would have found it difficult to withstand the shock. The experience proved a valuable one to the militiamen who were to be called out again more than once during the war."

Service records for Captain Hays' Company show most arrived at New York on August 22, 1776 and were discharged on September 25, 1776.

The Paymaster Rolls indicate they were paid from "the day of their arrival in New York, to the day of discharge, & allowing one day for every twenty miles travel to and from camp."

The decent men of Captain Hays' Company, 18th Regiment, acted no differently from the average militiaman then in service. They were primarily a home-guard force and because militiamen elected their own officers, these companies didn't have an effective chain of command. If there were pressing problems back at the farm or if it was harvest time, they took off at will. Because of their hunting skills, in the early battles they were better at shooting from behind trees and stonewalls than fighting in a standing formation.

These patriotic men were called to a duty beyond their training to fight battle-seasoned troops. History shows that after this stumbling start in 1776, the Militia stepped up in later battles and after proper training using Baron Von Steuben's techniques, they became disciplined and effective soldiers who contributed greatly to the successful outcome of the war.

Men who made a difference

Tudor Holcomb

James Lee Loomis

William Mills Maltbie

Theodore "Thede" Case.
SBHS photos.

In the late 1800s and early 1900s, the small farming community of Granby nurtured many young men who later became influential in the affairs of state, town and business.

One of these was Tudor Holcomb to whom we are indebted for the gift of the Holcomb Farm in West Granby. Tudor Holcomb also built the present Granby Town Hall, gave land to the West Granby firehouse, land and money to the West Granby Methodist Church and donated land for a small park in West Granby.

James Lee Loomis was the product of Granby's one-room schoolhouse system. His college years at Yale University and Yale Law School prepared him to become President of the Connecticut Mutual Life Insurance Company in Hartford. He lived his entire life in Granby where he continued the family tradition of community service.

Another native son, Chief Justice of the State of Connecticut Supreme Court William Mills Maltbie, lived in the house just south of the Dutch Iris B&B on "The Street" in Granby center and was active in town affairs all of his life.

The trappings of law also attached themselves to Judge Theodore Case who went by the nickname "Thede." The Case family home faces the north side of the Granby Green on the corner of Route 20 and Salmon Brook Street.

George Seymour Godard (June 17, 1865 to February 12, 1936) was born at 58 Granville Road in North Granby, just past Silver Street on the right. As a young man, Godard applied himself to his studies and graduated from Wilbraham Academy in 1886. He received his AB from Wesleyan University in 1892, a BD from Yale in 1893, an honorary MA from Wesleyan in 1916, an honorary MA from Trinity in 1919 and an honorary DLitt from Wesleyan in 1935.

During his early years at Wesleyan, he took courses under Woodrow Wilson who later became President of the United States.

George Seymour Godard, 1865-1936. W. S. Hart photo

In 1890, Godard took a year off from college to supervise construction of the Cossitt Library in North Granby. He became its first librarian and married his assistant, Kate Estelle Dewey, on June 23, 1897.

In 1898, Connecticut State Librarian Charles J. Hoadley, recognized Godard's abilities and hired him as Assistant Librarian. When Hoadley died in 1900, Godard assumed the top office. At that time the State Library was housed in the State Capitol Building.

The library soon outgrew its limited quarters, and Godard was instrumental in the planning and construction of the State Library and Supreme Court Building on Capitol Avenue in Hartford. Much of the interior reflects Godard's ideas.

The library archives contain many personal papers relating to Godard's life. One unusual item is a handwritten letter from his mother, Sabara Lavinia Beach Godard. The letter, dated December 9, 1877, was written to George's brother, Oren Harvy Godard. George was twelve years old and very ill with a fever.

Good Evening Oren,

How do you do? Well I trust—and getting along nicely. Your roomates the same. George is no worse. We think much better though his fever has not yet "turned" and we have nothing to calculate from as the fever was about him undoubtedly for some days before we came home.

Doct. Cutler is doing well for all his patients and establishing a reputation as a first class physician in fevers at least in fact he is gaining the confidence of his townspeople in general and seems to be the people's choice. They seem never to think how "wild" he has been.

Poor Georgie is nearly "done up" in onions—on his feet—under his arms and across his stomach—chopped onions—besides plates of the savory vegetable standing about the room—in addition to this prescription of Hamy's he is washed thoroughly in saleratus water and rubbed in highwines twice a day. So you see no common fever can last long with such treatment as that. The Doct. says he is doing as well as can be expected as he was very bad when he came home.

Alonzo Holcomb (Bushy Hill) fell from a tobacco scaffolding in his barn on Monday last and lay insensible about 46 hours and is now in a very critical condition. Mrs. Booth (Starling Reed's mother) has a stroke of paralysis.

Mother and Soplua took Ollie home with them Friday night. Miss Griswold is not able to commence her school this week on account of rheumatism. Miner called to see Georgie this evening and inquired about you. He said he intended to have written to you before now. I gave him your address. Frank B. brought your rooster home from the barn as the fellow used to come to his house and half kill his rooster and he could not "stand it" any longer so he "toted" the gentleman down to the grist mill as Harvy didn't want any battles here. Wells and Dea Dewey are again indulging in a free fight with half the town as witnesses. Came for Harvy to attend their court at Hftd. tomorrow but he declined as he had not taken interest enough in the affair to do them any good. Well here I am at the end of this sheet of paper. I am scribbling this on a book in my lap while I'm watching with Georgie.

Good night, Mother

A large oil portrait of George Seymour Godard hangs over the first floor entrance at the Cossitt Library. He is forever remembered with a plaque imbedded in rock at the corner of Granville Road and Godard Road. On a cold and drizzly Sunday afternoon in 1936, Governor Wilbur Snow, with other state dignitaries in attendance, made the dedication. The inscription is as follows:

"In Memoriam, George Seymour Godard, State Librarian, 1900-1936.
Born near this spot which he loved, no man served more loyally or performed more perfectly the duties of his trust."

Sinnamon was lucky

About half way down driveway B in the Granby Center cemetery, is the gravestone of Mary Godard Hadley and Sinnamon. Sinnamon's life span was three years shorter than that of Hadley. Sinnamon was fortunate because his foster family contributed greatly to the growth of Granby. Sinnamon was influenced in his early years by the Hartford Public School System and later attended Lasell Junior College in Newton, Massachusetts.

Sinnamon was a Teddy Bear young Mary Godard received on her third birthday. The bear was her lifetime companion, and Sinnamon's ashes lie with Mary's in this plot.

In 1902, a Washington Post political cartoon depicted President Theodore Roosevelt refusing to shoot an American black bear cub his companions had tracked and treed while hunting in Mississippi. Morris Michtom, an entrepreneurial candy-store owner in Brooklyn had a toy bear made to sell in his store. Michtom sent Roosevelt one of the bears and received permission to use the President's nickname "Teddy," for the toy. He displayed the small bear in his shop window with a sign that read "Teddy's Bear." Teddy Bears are still in demand today, and people of all ages can tell you about the bears they had as kids.

Life magazine, on December 11, 1970, published pictures of several people with their early teddy bears. Mary Godard Hadley, at age sixty-seven, was pictured sitting in her home with Sinnamon—her companion, playmate and confessor all those many years.

During his 73-year existence, Sinnamon learned that the patriarch of the family, Daniel Gozzard, came from England and had roots in Hartford in 1646. His son, Nicholas Gozzard, went over the mountain to Simsbury and records show that in 1677 he owned thirty acres of land on the northwest side of the Barn Door Hills in present-day West Granby. On page 48 of his book, "Tempest in a Small Town," Mark Williams noted that in 1688 the first settlers of future Granby owned nine lots. The Salmon Brook Historical Society now stands on what was Lot 7. Three lots south was old Nicholas Gozzard.

Mary Godard Hadley traced her lineage to Revolutionary War veteran, Moses Godard, her great-great-great grandfather (1746-1832). He served in Captain Hays' Company of the Granby Militia, which joined the 18th Regiment under Colonel Jonathan Pettibone of Simsbury. Digging deeper, however, shows Moses was in service from August 23, 1776, to September 20, 1776, just one month. By August 27 other troops had lost the battle for Long Island, and General Washington requested Connecticut send militia to hold the Island of Manhattan.

Private Moses Godard was on shore with Hays on September 15 when British forces struck at Kip's Bay, about where 34th Street is today. The militia units turned tail and ran. General Washington himself tried to halt the retreat but to no avail. History books record this as the Panic at Kip's Bay. Moses' grave in West Granby Cemetery is decorated with a small American flag each Memorial Day.

Mrs. Hadley's grandfather, Harvy (with no "e") Godard (1823-1896), was born and died in the brown house just past Silver Street on Granville Road in North Granby. He served in the Connecticut General Assembly and was the first Grand Master of the Connecticut Grange when it was founded in 1875. He was also Master of Granby Grange #5 from 1875-1893.

George O. Beach, Mrs. Hadley's great uncle, was a founder of the Granby Creamery. He owned and operated the farm now known as Allen's Cider Mill in North Granby.

George Seymour Godard (1866-1936) was the most prominent member of the Godard family. He became the first Librarian of Cossitt Library in 1890 and served as the Connecticut State Librarian from 1900-1936. On the rocky corner of Godard Road and Granville Road across from the Crag, the State of Connecticut, in 1937, mounted an engraved bronze plaque that states: "In memoriam, George Seymour Godard, State Librarian, 1900-1936. Born near this spot which he loved, no man served more loyally or performed more perfectly the duties of his trust."

Books 2, 3 and 4 of the Granby land records burned. Surviving volumes from 1786, when Granby was incorporated, have 706 entries for the Godard name. Today, not one person lives in town whose name is spelled Godard.

Yes, Sinnamon was lucky. If he could have spoken, he might have used President Teddy Roosevelt's favorite expression—"Bully"—to describe his life.

WHEN GRANBY WAS YOUNG

Granby nostalgia—
A presentation to the Salmon Brook Historical Society

In 1991 I spoke to members of the Salmon Brook Historical Society. The group gathered in the Cooley Schoolhouse that had recently been moved to the society grounds. The evening was chilly, and a fire was lit in the potbelly stove. With a lecture and slide show, I described the *Granby as I knew in the 1920s and 1930s.*

The Salmon Brook Historical Society, Granby, Connecticut.
Peter Dinella photo

In the center of town, the Loomis Brothers Store stood at the old intersection of Hartford Avenue and Salmon Brook Street. It was also the

Town Clerk's Office. Across Hartford Avenue, an old time emporium, Avery's General Store, sold clothing, hardware and food. In the same building, the center Post Office occupied what is now JD's barbershop. Down Hartford Avenue, in the old Beman Building, Maynard Holcomb ran a soda fountain that was later taken over by Harold Cotton. Farther east, across the railroad tracks, Walter Simmons ran a grain and feed business and, next door, Tracy Crouse and Bill Bertini owned Granby Supply, a building supply store. Peter L. Brown occupies that building today.

Granby Depot was an active place where steam trains whistled in and out at all hours. Around World War I it was not easy to get to Hartford, twenty miles away, as the automobile had not come into wide use. My mother, Grace Minerva, took a wagon or rode a horse down to Tariffville, put the horse in the livery and boarded the train that went through Bloomfield and into Union Station at Hartford. The other choice was to ride through East Granby to the Rainbow section of Poquonock and take the trolley in.

Families went to Hartford frequently for shopping, dentist or doctor appointments and banking, as well as for entertainment. Old diaries tell of dining at the old Honiss Oyster House where the walls were hung with portraits of the famous, and then to a live performance at the Parsons Theater that stood where the Phoenix glass-boat building is today.

On the corner of Salmon Brook Street and Pendleton Road, the gold Victorian house with its second floor solarium windows was built in the late 1800s. During the 1920s Dr. Ernest R. Pendleton made it his home. He also maintained a medical practice and a small hospital there until the early 1940s. Pendleton built and owned the Salmon Brook Golf Course that lay partly on the land that is now Salmon Brook Park.

Up Salmon Brook Street by Cranberry Pond, where my Grandma Lena used to pick cranberries, the Forsyth family ran a sawmill and a gristmill. Today the buildings house the furniture and gift shops called Old Mill Pond Village.

The American Legion Hall on North Granby Road was originally a Universalist Church. In the 1930s it became a two-room schoolhouse with eight grades. Prior to 1958 Granby did not have a high school. Granby teens were tuition students at Simsbury High School in the brownstone building in Simsbury Center that now houses the Town of Simsbury municipal offices.

Loomis Brothers' Store

The Loomis Brothers store in the late 1800s. SBHS photo

Most people who moved to Granby after 1975 will not recall the building depicted here.

Even though there were several owners of the structure, most people still usually refer to it as Loomis Brothers. It was built in 1891 and razed in 1975 and was located on the southeast corner of Hartford Avenue (Rte. 189) and Salmon Brook Street (Rte. 10) at the present signal lights.

Through at least half of its existence the old store was the center of everyday life for the small farming populace of Granby.

Over time it housed the founder's general store and included the town offices, the circuit court, a barbershop in the basement, and on the second floor, an apartment that was later the meeting place for the St. Mark's Mason Lodge.

Back in 1896, when telephone service came to town, Loomis Brothers was quick to sign up for installation. Their number was (eight-ring-two). Now a customer was able to call ahead to determine whether or not an item was in stock. Prior to this convenience, he had hitched up the horse and wagon and driven to town, maybe from some miles away, only to learn the desired article was not in stock.

Looking back to the 1940s, I recall getting my fishing license at the Town Clerk's office. With nostalgia, I also recall a cold winter's night when I visited the lodge to see Phil Devenew receive his fifty-year pin. The potbellied stove in the center of the room gave off a circle of welcome heat in that uninsulated, wooden structure with loose fitting windows.

In the recesses of my mind is a memory of the 1930s when a dusty dull-maroon Mack bus made occasional stops for passengers going to and from the New England Transportation terminal at Union Station in Hartford. The ancient bus was a big improvement over the early 1900s when travel was by stagecoach from this same spot.

In its heydays, Loomis Brothers was truly a general store. It carried groceries, meats, fish, hardware, farm machinery, clothing, dry goods, horse blankets, kerosene, liniments, overalls, gloves, shoes, boots, bicycles, candy, fertilizers, suspenders, stationery, pens, ink, writing paper, and much more.

With its multiple occupants, the building drew most everyone it town, at one time or another, to its doors. People could certainly catch up on local news and gossip for they came here from all levels of society.

Loomis Brothers went back many years before this building was erected in 1891. It all started in 1856 when the two brothers, Chester P. and James N. Loomis, opened a store directly across the street from the pictured site.

Their Yankee pluck paid off and business was prosperous for many years until, in 1876, they were burned out. Undaunted, the brothers moved into an existing building on the opposite side of the street. Prosperity followed, and they remained there until 1891 when they constructed a new edifice to their specifications.

The years brought many changes. In 1935 a Red and White Store replaced the Loomis Brothers store, and in 1947 Guay and Kellogg took over the operation.

The final distancing from the founders took place in 1975 when the Connecticut Department of Transportation announced that the intersection of Routes 189 and 202/10 was slated for realignment. The old store was razed to make way for a new, straight intersection and traffic lights. A property swap gave the Southern New England Telephone switching office and Tanner's gas station (Food Bag) access to the new road and also added a strip of land to the south end of the Green. Loomis Brothers Store stood about sixty feet east of Route 10 under the present Route 189.

The Loomis Brothers store building at the intersection of
Routes 189 and 2020/10 just before it was razed in 1975.
Today Route 189 passes over the old store site. SBHS photo

Over the past 150 years, many small New England towns have reared
people like the Loomis brothers; men who did similar things to advance
a town's growth. However, these two stalwarts were Granby's own. I'm
certain their mutual ingenuity and perseverance leave us with a much
warmer impression than say—Wal-Mart!

Cragg Mill, North Granby

The old Cragg Mill in North Granby.
Pen & ink drawing by W. S. Hart

This pen and ink sketch of the Cragg gristmill was done from a photo taken a few weeks before the catastrophic flood in August 1955. The mill was located in North Granby, which abuts the state line at Granville, Massachusetts to the north and the Southwick Jog to the east. Five miles south of Granville, on Route 189, the east branch of Salmon Brook drops through a deep gorge called the Crag. Over 200 years ago, the brook was damned above the gorge to form a millpond.

The *Heritage Of Granby*, on page 99, notes that: "In December of 1794, it was voted at a town meeting, that Marten Gossard (Goddard) may build a gristmill on his own land." This was probably the Cragg Mill that was built on the north branch of the Salmon Brook at the juncture of North Granby Road and Silver Street."

Two errors in that statement need to be corrected. First, the location is at Silver Street's juncture with Granville Road, not North Granby Road.

The second error takes a little more doing. A search of old deeds indicates that the mill was there in May of 1757 and owned by James Hillyer. Several deeds refer to one quarter, one third and one half interests held by other people and businessmen in the community.

Eva Dewey, Curator Emeritus of the Salmon Brook Historical Society, researched the mill's beginnings, and her notes on file at the historical society show the mill being there as early as 1776. She also found that Thomas Copley (1743-1797) left his interest in the mill to his widow and daughters. Two of the daughters married Gossards, and over the years, ownership of the mill property passed to Harvy Godard, (1823-1896).

Harvy Godard's estate was settled by his sons, George Seymour and Fred Munyon Godard who acted as administratorsThey sold the gristmill to Mary C. Place and her husband for $500 on May 18,1898.

On August 23, 1915, Mary Place sold it back into the Godard family through Porter B. Godard, (1861-1943) for $200. On July 6, 1942, Porter B. Godard gave the mill property to his nephew and namesake, Porter B. Godard. On December 27, 1977, Porter B. Godard gave it to his nephew William S. Hart.

The original log dam.

Wooden bridge at Silver Street.

Cragg Mill viewed
from the gorge.

Mill from the Silver
Street bridge.

When Harvy Godard died in 1896, the old mill ceased regular operation. It was, however, capable of grinding grain until 1915 when the log dam was replaced with concrete and the old wooden bridge by a steel structure. The concrete foundation and retaining wall to support the new bridge completely blocked and filled the sluiceway between the millpond and the mill. The catastrophic flood of 1955 lifted the old mill from its foundations and swept it downstream.

Mill site the day after the 1955 flood viewed from the gorge.

Remains of the mill's foundation the day after the 1955 flood.
W. S. Hart photos

The structure did not have a familiar water wheel attached to the exterior of the building. As did most New England mills, the Cragg mill utilized a tub wheel located inside the building. The tub wheel was run by a head of water directed through a sluiceway from the millpond and under Silver Street to make a ten-foot drop into a tall, circular tub fitted with a rotating, finned wheel set in the horizontal position. Its perpendicular shaft extended upwards from the moving wheel and, through a series of wooden-toothed gears, turned the grindstones to produce the meal.

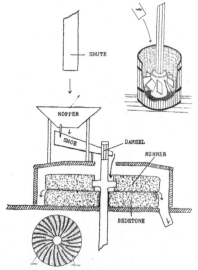

A tub wheel, the grinding mechanism and a mill wheel.

The log dam was strong enough to hold back the tons of water in the pond. To prevent seepage, large vertical planks were placed side by side against the logs. The mill operated only when the millpond was full. When the pond level dropped below the sluiceway, the mill shut down until the pond refilled.

The tub wheel had a large advantage over the external wheel. An external-wheel mill shut down when the millpond froze and remained idle all winter. But, because the tub wheel drew water from below the frozen surface of the pond, it could operate all year round

Grain brought to the mill by local farmers was hauled with a rope and pulley to the top floor and stored in large bins. As the grain was needed, it dropped through wood chutes to hoppers above the grindstones.

The bottom stone, or "bedder," did not turn because it was permanently bedded into the floor. The bedder had a large hole in its center through which the drive shaft extended to turn the upper stone called the "runner." The runner could be lifted to adjust the coarseness of the meal or to prevent wear on the wheels when not in use. The miller always maintained a very small tolerance between the wheels to prevent direct contact that could create sparks and ignite the fine dust created by the milling process.

A "damsel" at the top of the rotating shaft meted out small amounts of grain from the overhead hopper. The flat sides of the damsel tapped a shoe suspended under the hopper, which released grain through the center hole of the upper stone to the surface of the lower stone. As the upper stone rotated, it ground the grain, and by means of a series of lands and furrows, worked it to the outer edges where it was collected and funneled into bags.

The lands and furrows dulled with use. An itinerant stone dresser sharpened them using a hammer and metal pick to chip the stones. Tiny pieces of metal became imbedded in the back of his hand as he chipped away. In the next town, he might be asked to prove his qualifications when the miller said, "Show us your metal, mate."

When a Frenchman named Fourneyron invented the metal turbine wheel in 1827, wood tub mills and exterior wheel mills became obsolete. Many rural mills continued to operate for many years, but eventually the turbine dominated the industry. Progress pushed the old mills aside, just as it did crude blast furnaces, steam locomotives, trolleys and the old family farm.

Sources: "The Mill," by Janice Tyrwhitt, printed by New York Graphic Society, Boston. "Early American Mills," by Martha and Murray Zimiles, printed by Bramhall House, New York.

Granby's forgotten creamery

Granby Creamery on Creamery Hill Road as seen from the street.
It was located at 62 Creamery Hill where private barns stand today. SBHS photo

Throughout New England, from the 1870s to the 1940s, the local creamery contributed to the farming economy. Creameries served the local farmers for decades before modern dairy processing plants slowly and quietly replaced them. Their history reminds me of my grandfather's old saying: "Every dog has its day."

Finding written history of the Granby Creamery turned out to be futile. I was able to gather some insight through the discovery of a paragraph here and there, and from anecdotes local historians had gleaned from individuals who recalled the creameries.

After the Civil War small dairy farms became more common in rural New England. In addition to selling the milk, farmers' wives made cheese and butter and sold or bartered what the family didn't use. Butter was, and still is, made from cream. To separate the cream, whole milk was poured into large shallow pans or other containers. The cream rose to the surface and was skimmed off.

The majority of farmers bred their herds to freshen the cows for milking during the spring, summer and fall months, and allowed them to go dry over the winter. In the 1870s and 1880s, farmers began storing enough hay to last the winter and supplemented it with grain. The silo became popular, and corn ensilage came into its own as winter feed. Cream became available year-round, but quality and freshness varied from farm to farm.

It became increasingly practical for dairy farmers to form a share-holding creamery association and build a centralized creamery. Milk was gathered from its members, the butter churned at one location and distributed to a common market.

The Swedish invention of a centrifugal cream separator in 1882 was a boon to the butter industry. The separator processed large quantities of milk to obtain the cream in considerably less time. By the end of the century, a smaller, refined machine manufactured by De Laval made it possible for a farmer to have his own.

Volume and butterfat content determined how much a farmer was paid for his milk. Jersey and Guernsey cows were noted for high butterfat milk. Holsteins were large-volume milkers, but produced low butterfat.

Until the discovery of a fairly simple testing process, it was difficult to determine the percentage of butterfat in milk. Arguments over whether it should be measured by the inch or by volume were common. This quotation from "The Hill Country of New England" by Harold Fisher, explains the process that resolved those arguments:

> "In 1890 the Babcock Tester was developed. The milk sample, from each farmer, was mixed with an equal quantity of sulfuric acid, which dissolved the casein and set the butterfat free. The

mixture was placed in the machine and spun for five minutes. Water was then added and a consequent whirling forced the butterfat into the graduated neck of the testing bottle, making it easy to measure the percentage of fat."

Babcock's machine, a hand-cranked centrifuge that removed air bubbles from the butterfat and introduction of a standardized measurement, assured farmers of fair compensation for their milk and the creamery of consistent butter quality. In later years, butterfat testing influenced breeding considerations for dairy farmers wanting to produce milk with a higher fat content.

Granby had a creamery at 62 Creamery Hill Road. Over the sixty-odd years since it ceased operation, the old creamery buildings have disappeared and presently a privately owned cow barn stands on the site.

The Salmon Brook Historical Society has a taped interview with Harold Cotton, now deceased, who recalled working in the creamery as a boy in 1904—four years before Henry Ford put his Model T into production in 1908. From Mr. Cotton's description, and those of others, the Granby Creamery was typical of most butter making operations.

With no electricity or waterpower, a steam engine ran the machinery. The facility housed a boiler room and just outside was a shed for coal or wood to fire the boiler.

Cream gatherers in wagons pulled by horse teams, traveled from farm to farm over dirt roads. The cream, in fifty-gallon barrels, was hauled back to the creamery. There, a rope and pulley wheel hoisted the barrels to the second floor where the cream was poured into chutes that emptied into four-hundred-gallon vats on the ground floor. Tubes ran from the vats to the butter churn.

> In a note written in May of 1975, Arthur Clark said:
> "I can still see just how the creamery looked inside. There was a big churn suspended between two axles and rotated by power from a steam engine. After the cream was churned into butter, it was placed on a rotating table (also steam powered) where a man worked salt into the butter (one ounce to one pound) with a long paddle. Next the butter was pressed into one-pound wooden molds then pushed out and wrapped in parchment paper."

Harold Cotton recalled that the churn was large enough for him to get his head and shoulders inside to scrape out all the butter.

To prevent bacteria growth, there was a washroom next to the boiler room where hot water and steam were readily available to sanitize the paddles and other implements.

In summer, refrigeration was a problem. Helen Howland, of Granby, recalled:

> " . . . ingenuity took care of that when the creamery was built. At the end of the building was a high bank. A room was built surrounded by the bank, built in cement, top, sides and floor, with no windows. That room was so cold, summer and winter, that the temperature was always forty degrees or below. A heavy, heavy door closed the room. You shivered when you entered it."

To keep summer shipments cold, an icehouse was filled with blocks of local ice during the winter and packed in sawdust to last the summer. The icehouse had double plank walls with the gap between them stuffed with sawdust for insulation. This type of icehouse presented a fire hazard. Fresh sawdust sometimes fermented into wood alcohol and, if the summer was hot enough, spontaneous combustion could set the sawdust and the building on fire.

One-pound cakes of butter were stacked on wooden trays and shipped in wooden boxes. In the center of each shipment, a section equivalent to two pounds of butter was replaced with a zinc container filled with ice. Shipping boxes came in varying sizes, and buyers that wanted to buy in bulk could purchase tubs holding up to fifty pounds.

Buttermilk was a by-product of churning, and for a while it was shipped to saloons and restaurants in ten-gallon cans. However, for a few cents a barrel, most of the butterfat was sold back to the farmers to feed livestock.

Granby Creamery had an unusual coal supply situation. Once a week they bought a train carload of coal that was delivered to the siding at Granby Depot some five miles away. The coal had to be unloaded within two days or they would be charged rent on the coal car. Local farmers pitched in with their teams and wagons and made several trips between the depot and the creamery shed each week.

The Granby Co-Operative Creamery was started on July 3, 1882. One of its organizers, George O. Beach, owned the farm now known as

Allenhurst, diagonally across from the Cossitt Library in North Granby. The original Italianate house burned several years ago and a modern one-story house replaced it.

Mr. Beach was elected president of the creamery and also served as president of the Granby Agricultural Society. He had also served in the Connecticut Legislature.

In 1882, the creamery buildings, equipment and tools cost $4,154.65. At the height of business, in 1906, the association manufactured 206,000 pounds of butter. Receipts of $40,000 were distributed among the Granby shareholders.

By the late 1930s, as with most small creameries, changing dairy trends forced the Granby Creamery to sell to Miller's Milk, a large dairy in Bloomfield some ten miles away.

The taken-for-granted ice cube

In the 1920s and 1930s not everyone had electricity. Without an electric refrigerator, perishable food was stored in a zinc-lined wooden icebox cooled by a large cake of ice in a compartment at the top of the box.

On our family farm, as with others, the ice from local ponds was harvested in the dead of winter. If the harvest was large enough, it supplied us through to July before it ran out. Our source was the family millpond.

Vernon Jenkins and James J. Thompson cutting ice
February 1936. SBHS photo

A workhorse, with sharp cleats attached to its shoes for traction, pulled a five-foot-long upright cutting blade that scored a straight line in the ice the length of the pond. At the end of each pass across the pond, the blade was moved twenty-four inches and another line was cut. With these cuts as guidelines, smaller block sizes were marked off. A man cut along the scored lines to break the ice into smaller blocks using a four-foot ice saw with a perpendicular wooden handle. He stood over the line and worked the blade up and down in what seemed like an endless task.

The ice blocks were loaded onto a sturdy wagon and hauled to the icehouse. Typically the icehouse was twenty-feet long by fifteen-feet wide by ten-feet high. The ice was packed with sawdust between the blocks to prevent them from forming one huge mass when some melting took place.

Icehouses were a fire hazard. For insulation purposes, the exterior walls of the structure were of double thickness. Plank walls were spaced a foot apart and the void filled with sawdust to keep the cold in and the heat out. If the sawdust was dry, there was no problem. However, sometimes it was fresh sawdust from the nearby sawmill. As with all vegetation, wood goes through a fermentation process that produces wood alcohol. On occasion, fermentation took place between the walls, and by spontaneous combustion, the house caught on fire. A similar hazard occurs when improperly cured hay is stored in a barn.

The ice industry was huge. To supply the cities and to meet local needs, ice was cut from every sizeable body of fresh water. Working for a large New York ice company, hundreds of men harvested 220,000 tons of ice a year from Congamond Ponds in Southwick, Massachusetts, and stored it in five huge icehouses. It was the largest ice operation in the state. The men worked from December through February in bitter cold conditions.

The heavy work required a large number of horses. Some years ago, an old timer told me that in the 1920s he was hired to look after the horses. It took several men to feed, groom, clean the stalls, maintain harnesses and tend to the illnesses and injuries of those animals.

He also said heavy drinking was one of the big problems of working at the ponds. The men worked from sunrise to sundown. With little entertainment, they were bored in the evening. Apparently the best way to relax was with liquor. My friend quit the job because he worried that he might become a drunk.

The horse-drawn ice wagon was a common sight in the villages and cities. From late spring through early fall, a housewife placed a square white card with a number printed on it in a front window. On ice day when the ice wagon pulled up in front of a house, the driver knew from the number what size chunk the woman needed. Most icemen had well-developed biceps and wore sleeveless leather vests. He used an ice pick to break off the block and grabbed it with large iron tongs. With the block on his shoulder, he went around the house, through the back door and deposited the block in the icebox.

While he was away from the wagon, neighborhood children (me included) jumped up on the back step and grabbed splinters of ice to suck on. When the driver came back, he hollered at us and we ran like crazy. Undoubtedly he found our routine amusing, because he probably did the same thing in his youth.

Tobacco—a cash crop

Hauling a load of field tobacco to the barn. SBHS photo

A few years ago, the Hartford *Courant* published an article profiling the towns in the Farmington Valley, an area of approximately a twenty-five mile radius. In the entire area, there were only twenty-five farms with a total of one thousand and thirty-nine cows. Granby was listed as having only six farms. Fifty years ago there were probably six farms to the mile.

In addition to family farms there were several shade tobacco growers. Shade grown was an economic mainstay of the Connecticut River Valley, and the cured leaves were prized as premium cigar wrappers. The delicate leaf needed protection from the sun and a humid environment. Gauzy white netting covered hundreds of acres across the Connecticut River Valley, and those fields resembled huge lakes when viewed from the air.

Among the large independent growers was Fred Colton on Salmon Brook Street. His daughter Mildred's husband, Nate Allison, later took over the operation. The tobacco shed at the Salmon Brook Historical Society was built by Colton. In West Granby, Tudor Holcomb grew tobacco as well as running a large dairy business. On Hungary Road, Charles Griffin grew forty-two acres of tobacco.

The large corporate growers such as Culbro Brothers and the American Sumatra Company bussed kids in daily from the inner city to work in the fields and paid them twenty-five cents an hour. Those growers also hired Jamaicans, paid for their travel to Connecticut and Massachusetts and fed and housed them in barracks and dormitories in several valley towns. The companies held back part of the men's pay each week, and gave it to them as a lump sum in the fall when they returned home to their families.

Most teenagers worked in tobacco. Tobacco and other agricultural jobs were about all that was available for teens in the 30s, 40s and 50s. If you didn't live on a farm, the labor-intense tobacco fields offered a job and pocket money.

Shade grown tobacco plants were started from seed, thinned and nurtured in hot beds in the spring. When the weather was right and the seedlings the correct size, they were transplanted into the fields in long rows from a horse- or tractor-drawn flatbed.

Posts that supported the tents stood at regular intervals down the length and breadth of the field. The tenting was repaired or replaced each spring. The posts divided the rows into "bents," which were a measure of labor during the picking season.

Under the tenting, the plants needed almost constant care. As the stalk grew and a leaf stemmed from it, a small growth called a sucker grew at the juncture of the two. Suckers were removed by hand. Imagine how many suckers on a plant, how many rows an acre and how many acres involved, and you'll understand how labor intensive growing tobacco is. The fields were kept free of weeds with hoes.

The leaves on the bottom of the plant matured first. When these were of size, the hands, in three-man teams, worked four rows at a time under the tenting. One dragged a rectangular canvas basket along the center aisle to gather the leaves picked by the other two. Only the first three leaves from the bottom of the stalk were taken in the first picking. A few days went by and the next leaves up the stalk were ready to pick. There were usually three or four pickings over the course of the season. The last small leaves were left, and the tasseled top of the plant poked up into the netting by late August.

The canvas baskets filled with handpicked leaves were taken to long sheds that stretched along the edges of the fields. Each leaf was hand sewn onto a string threaded through a heavy needle. The women who did the sewing used heavy, usually homemade, leather palm guards to protect their hands. The heel of the hand was used to drive the needle through the thick fibrous stalks. When full, the string was attached to a tobacco lath, which was handed up to men who climbed into the barn's rafters to hang them from the top downward in tiers. This allowed air to circulate to dry and cure the leaves.

Many family farms, such as ours, had a tobacco shed and grew some open field tobacco as a money crop. Some large growers also cultivated field tobacco. Field tobacco wasn't a fine wrapper leaf; it was chopped up to become cigar filler.

William S. Hart Sr. and a team headed for the tobacco barn at the North Granby farm in the summer of 1917. W. S. Hart photo

Field tobacco was exposed to the elements and was a coarser, thicker leaf. The entire plant was harvested in August. The plant was cut off close to the ground, and the stem speared onto a lath with a detachable metal spear on its end. Several stalks were speared on each lath and loaded onto an odd looking wagon with parallel wooden rails that ran its length. The lath rested on the rails with the leaves hanging down. The metal spear was put onto another lath and the process repeated. When the wagon was full, the load was drawn to the shed where the tobacco-laden laths were hung for curing.

The leaves cured over a period of several weeks. The sheds had vertical-plank siding, and every third plank (slat) was hinged at the top so it could be propped open with a foot-long wrought iron hook. At first, the green tobacco was full of moisture that needed to be removed as fast as possible. To do this, the slats were closed and charcoal fires in metal containers were placed the length the shed to draw the moisture out. With the initial moisture removed the fires were put out, and the slats opened to allow air circulation to do the rest. In a very damp or rainy season when mildew and rotting became a concern, the sheds were closed and the fires restarted.

When the leaves were properly cured, the lath was handed down and each leaf stripped by hand. The delicate shade grown leaves were placed in cases for shipping to the processing warehouse. The field-grown leaf was wrapped in bundles and shipped to warehouses in Hartford.

A tie to the past

Through the years I have been drawn to the tile-roofed Mansard-style building at 255 Salmon Brook Street in the center of Granby. It's owned by the Guarco family and is divided into apartments.

My mother, Grace Godard Hart, recalled that one of our ancestors, Miles Godard Gaines, ran a hotel in that building.

Carol Laun, Archivist and Genealogist for the Salmon Brook Historical Society, researched the early days of the site, and her information was incorporated into an excellent and informative article done by Tom Chesney in the July 1997 edition of the Granby *Drummer*. With that great foundation, I pursued the history further.

The structure is one of the few in town with this architectural design. I spoke with a contractor doing some restoration there and learned it is a plank house that was built with a dirt-floored cellar. Foundation walls are fieldstone to ground level, with brick for about a foot and a half to support the building's sills.

The old builders used planks that were two or three inches thick and ten- to twelve-inches wide and nailed them lengthwise to the sill and to the second floor "rim joist." The second floor was built in the same manner. Lath for plaster completed the interior walls. The exterior was sheathed and usually sided with clapboards.

When running water and electricity became available, plank houses did not accommodate running pipes and wiring through the walls. It was common in a plank house for the pipes and wiring to run from the basement to the second floor in a corner of a first floor room.

The house in Granby center was built around 1880 to replace one that had burned in February 1877 along with the Post Office and Loomis Brother's Store. The store moved across the street to an existing building, and in 1891 the Loomis brothers built the structure that stood at the intersection of Route 189 and Salmon Brook Street until it was razed in 1975.

The Gaines Hotel. A pen & ink drawing by W. S. Hart.

For history buffs, this is a list the owners, as shown in deeds, from 1778 to the present:

1788   Pliny Hillyer had a tavern on 25 acres
1822   Isaac Phelps
1839   Frederick Hayes
1855   Daniel Hayes as the Hayes Hotel
1858   Amasa Holcomb
1859   Charles Barnes as the Salmon Brook Hotel
1860   Milo Underhill as the tavern house
1864   Samuel Benjamin
1865   Charles Slocum
1867   Miles Godard Gaines
1873   Samuel Benjamin
1889   A.C. Green
1899   Edgar Case
1922   Widow Ina Case
1957   Estate of Ina Case
1982   Allesio Guarco
2000   Edward and David Guarco

Miles Godard Gaines (1834 to 1879) was named for his mother Nancy's father, Miles Godard. Miles lived at 20 Godard Road in North Granby and is buried in the Granby Center Cemetery. He once owned the old hotel that burned in 1877.

I think it interesting that young Miles married an Antionette Gibbons and his sister, Miranda Gaines, married a John Murray Gibbons. John, along with his father, Carlos, started the Gibbons cheese store in Granville, Massachusetts, in 1851. The original store burned in 1884. The new store burned in 1934, and today's quaint Colonial Revival building was built on the same site.

Miles was ambitious and not only ran the hotel, but also built a horse track at the rear of his twenty five acres where the Granby Town Hall stands. An 1869 map of Granby, available at the historical society, lists both the M. G. Gaines Hotel and the M. G. Gaines Trotting Park.

There is hearsay that Miles owned the hotel at the time of the February 1877 fire, and that he went broke trying to rebuild it. However, deeds show that Samuel Benjamin bought it in 1873, so Miles was out of it.

Miles did go broke. A December 20,1877, deed declared him an "insolvent debtor" as of August 5,1876. The Probate Court sold his dwelling place at 78 Donahue Road, North Granby to satisfy his debts. Could it be our Miles was unlucky at horses?

When I'm caught at the traffic light by 255 Salmon Brook Street, I can't help but wonder about the hopes and dreams of the 17 owners of this unique property.

Southwick: not the first jog

People living in towns abutting Southwick, Massachusetts have heard varying stories about how the jog in the Connecticut state line came to be.

It is interesting to me that the Southwick jog was not the first anomaly in the line between the two colonies. The colonies of Connecticut and Massachusetts, back in the 1630s, were in constant dispute about the common boundary line. People didn't know where they should pay their taxes, and even Springfield thought it was in the Colony of Connecticut.

In 1642 Massachusetts hired two surveyors, Nathaniel Woodward and Solomon Saffery, who laid out the boundary line that stood for decades. With the Massachusetts Charter as a guide they identified, as best they could, a starting point three miles south of the southernmost part of the Charles River. They boarded a ship and sailed up the Connecticut River to the find the matching latitude and drew a straight line on their map between the two points.

When completed, their map placed the line down by Bissell's Ferry at present day Windsor. This put Suffield and Enfield in Massachusetts Bay Colony. Connecticut disagreed with the outcome of their work, but didn't actively fight it.

Years later, in 1713, the colonies sought a compromise. A new survey placed the boundary line well north of the line Woodward and Saffrey had calculated seventy-one years earlier. It fell basically where it is today. The corrected line shifted Suffield and Enfield back within Connecticut boundaries.

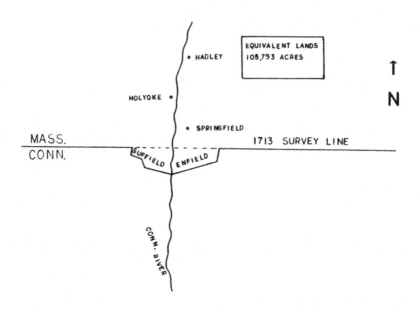

The 1713 line

A commission set up by the colonies was of the opinion that since the two towns had been started under the province of Massachusetts Bay Colony and paid taxes there, they would remain in Massachusetts. The commission further decided that because the Colony of Connecticut had lost this territory, Massachusetts would deed Connecticut an "equivalent" 105,793 acres of land. The land Massachusetts chose to give bordered the east side of Hadley, Massachusetts. Three years later Connecticut sold the land at auction to a Gurdon Saltonstall and several others for 683 pounds. The money was given to Yale College.

It becomes more interesting. In 1724, Suffield and Enfield residents, disgruntled by the earlier compromise, petitioned Connecticut to be brought into its jurisdiction. The General Assembly refused, saying the 1713 compromise should not be broken.

The request came up again in 1749, and this time Connecticut changed its mind, saying the 1713 decision had not been accepted by the English Crown and therefore was not binding. Suffield, Enfield and Woodstock were taken into the Colony of Connecticut.

Massachusetts was not pleased and continued to levy taxes on the towns. Meanwhile, the French & Indian War, the Tax Act and the Boston Massacre drew attention from the now hundred-year-long dispute. Nothing was settled.

Originally Westfield, Massachusetts included present day Southwick plus a similar amount of land east of the ponds that is now part of Suffield, Connecticut. In 1770, the people living in the southern part of Westfield broke away and called the new community Southwick. Four years later, in 1774, Southwick people living below the corrected 1713 Colony line petitioned the Connecticut General Assembly to become part of Connecticut.

Connecticut readily agreed, saying that Southwick west of the ponds would become part of Salmon Brook Society, a section of Simsbury. The area east of the ponds would be part of Suffield. This was great except the General Court of the Commonwealth of Massachusetts never agreed to it. The Revolution put the entire matter on hold for over a decade.

Southwick people west of the ponds apparently thought Connecticut's acceptance was good enough for them. When Salmon Brook Society broke away from Simsbury in 1786 to become The Town of Granby, they felt they were part of it. Evidence of this is that, with the exception of 1788 and 1789, two Southwick men—Roger and Reuben Moore—alternated as Listers for the town of Granby.

Granby Town Records of 1788 show the town acted on the Connecticut General Assembly's approval by delineating the borders between Granby and Suffield. The controversial Southwick land remained in Granby. It was decided that the Southwick—Granby town line followed the west side of the ponds north to where Two Mile Brook crosses the Massachusetts state line.

Those early people went happily on until 1803, when Massachusetts said: "Hold your horses! We never agreed to the 1774 petition approved by Connecticut." The wrangling continued until, in 1804, the two states met a compromise. The southern half of Southwick was divided at the lakes. The portion of Southwick west of the ponds would be part of Massachusetts, and that portion to the east would belong to Connecticut. Southwick would own the ponds. One hundred and sixty two years of uncertainty seemed to be resolved.

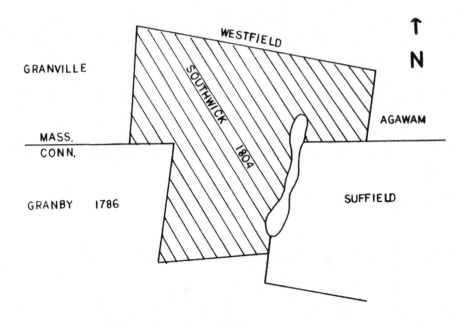

The 1804 line

But, guess what? Granby town records how that some nineteen years later, at a town meeting on May 6, 1823, people from the agreed-to Southwick presented a petition addressed to the Massachusetts General Court that was dated the last Wednesday of 1823. It requested that Southwick become a part of Connecticut. A 1999 search of the Massachusetts Archives in Boston found no record of the petition being presented.

It is final. You can rest comfortably knowing that the Southwick Jog is permanent and the myths have been put to rest.

How fortunate for future generations the heritage of these small towns is stored in the archives of our state libraries and historical societies and this type of history can be gleaned from them.

Connecticut boundary line moved again

The October 30, 1997, picture with this article is of a 1906 Connecticut/Massachusetts boundary marker that is located on the grounds of the Salmon Brook Historical Society in Granby.

A newcomer reading the engraving on the marker might think that Massachusetts is to the east. He or she could also assume that the adjacent Cooley Schoolhouse was built where it stands.

Backtracking to August 20, 1980, will help to clear up the puzzlement. On that date the schoolhouse was moved to the society grounds from its original location at the corner of Cooley Road and East Street in North Granby.

An 1855 Granby map didn't show a school located at that corner, however one was indicated on an 1863 map. Society archives indicate that two schools had stood on that site. The present Cooley School was built there in about 1870. Classes were held there until 1948 when a consolidated school system replaced the town's one- and two-room schools. A look at a Granby street map enables you to see what was unusual about the original school site.

In 1642 a border dispute between Connecticut and Massachusetts disrupted many early towns including Granby, Suffield, Woodstock and Southwick. It took over a century to resolve the issue. Massachusetts hired two surveyors, Woodward and Saffery, to establish the colony line. Over time, their line was disputed. The actual boundary was eight miles farther north.

The line was correctly surveyed in 1713, but it ran in a straight line with no notch or jog, even though many people living below the corrected line had settled old Westfield in Massachusetts. In 1770, the inhabitants of the lower section of Westfield broke away and became Southwick.

After 164 years of haranguing between the two states, an 1804 compromise created the present configuration, which gave the southern end of Southwick and the Congamond Ponds back to Massachusetts.

Final adjustments to the line were surveyed in 1906, and 165 granite markers were installed along the length of the border. To this day, the Survey Operations Section of the Connecticut Department of Transportation oversees the boundary and perambulates the line every five years.

At the original Cooley School location, a granite marker delineated the southwest corner of the Southwick jog. North Granby people probably weren't terribly pleased with that boundary decision. The schoolhouse was located in Connecticut, but the outhouse was in Massachusetts.

The Cooley School and its Massachusetts outhouse at
the corner of Cooley Road and East Street. SBHS photo

In 1994 a motor vehicle hit the marker and broke it off at ground level. The historical society communicated with the State of Connecticut, and in 1997, when it was determined that the stone couldn't be repaired, the marker was delivered to the society property.

Although the marker is turned ninety degrees from north to accommodate the school buildings' present location (facing west rather than south), you can still visualize the corner of the jog. History repeats itself and, symbolically, the outhouse remains in Massachusetts.

The ruin of Enders Forest

Thirty years of neglect by the Connecticut State Park and Forest Commission has made a ruin of Enders Forest located in the west end of the Granby.

This rural community enforces an open space plan in its development criteria. The Granby Land Trust holds large tracts of land donated by generous residents. Three families deserve special recognition for their unique contributions of land.

Tudor and Laura Holcomb's generosity created The Holcomb Farm with its 330-plus acres, a pristine house and outbuildings where the art center and ecology learning center serve the entire region. In addition, its

Community Supported Agriculture program grows thousands of pounds of vegetables for residents of Granby and Hartford.

A ride along Barn Door Hills Road, Simsbury Road and Salmon Brook Street takes one past the 4,800 acres of the McLean Game Refuge. Senator George P. McLean, also former Governor of Connecticut, created and endowed the refuge with his 1932 will. Parking areas and miles of walking trails are well maintained.

In contrast, the Ostrom Enders family gift of 1,035 acres in West Granby to the State of Connecticut is an ineffable failure. Granby Land Records (Volume 179, page 697) show that for one dollar, the large estate was quit claimed to the state on February 17, 1970. The wording of the deed, in part, is as follows:

"The premises herein described shall be maintained by the State Park and Forest Commission as a new and distinct State Forest and designated as the John Ostrom Enders and Harriet Whitman Enders State Forest, given the State by their children."

Thirty years ago, the property was very distinctive. A modest Saltbox house was in good repair as were the caretaker's cottage and two nearby barns. A small well house, with its rope and crank, stood in the middle of the mowed front lawn. Across the curve of the dirt road, a field of daffodils added beauty to the pastoral scene. Two hundred feet south, a cement dam with adjustable planks in its center sluiceway, controlled the water level of a picturesque pond.

The Ender's House and barns at its original location in
West Granby. W. S. Hart photo

Shortly after the state acquired the property, the Enders' Saltbox house was removed to the grounds of the Salmon Brook Historical Society in Granby center and was attached to the Abijah Rowe house (circa 1732). The Rowe house, the 1790s Weed-Enders House, the Cooley School and two other buildings are open for tours during the warmer months.

Today the Ender's House is part of the historical society's complex in Granby Center. Peter Dinella Photo

Sadly, that's where the nostalgia ends. Immediately after the house was moved, the state burned the caretaker's cottage and the adjacent barn. Another barn by the pond was dismantled for its boards and timbers.

As the years drifted by, a freshet washed out the earthworks abutting the cement dam and the pond drained. Over time alders grew in the opening left by the pond. Sometime in the late 1990s, someone put rocks into the dam opening and planks back into the sluiceway. Unfortunately, the alders were not cleared. Although the pond is full, the dead trunks and branches of the alders blight its surface.

In the 1970s the quiet dirt road was a pleasure to drive. Even more delightful was a hike along trails that passed stonewalls covered with blue-gray lichen and a small stream that gurgled and mingled with the birdcalls. A view of open green fields and, in season, beautiful foliage, extended the pleasure of this wonderful gift.

Today the road is pot-holed, washed out and difficult to walk. It mostly requires an off-road vehicle to traverse. A roadside area is used as a dumping ground. The public has long since dug up the daffodils.

Through the years, the Enders family maintained these acres to entertain Hartford bank, industrial and insurance executives. The pond was stocked with trout for those who liked to fly fish. Behind the caretaker's place, coops held pheasants that were released for the nimrods.

The Enders family raised beagles, and near the coops a well-maintained dog cemetery held many grave markers. One was a bronze medallion imbedded in a polished headstone that identified the final resting place of "Burnfoot Dazzle." The cemetery has been vandalized and the plot taken over by brush. Today, there is no evidence that the Enders treated their pet's remains with respect.

On Labor Day weekend in 1977, by the roadside near the park's entrance, the unidentified body of a murder victim was found. The crime remains unsolved; a Connecticut State Police cold case. With no surveillance or security, the park invites unsavory conduct, which scares hikers and nature lovers away.

Today, Enders Forest is a growing cancer destroying what remains of a piece of Granby's heritage. Perhaps town officials should demand that the Park and Forest Commission live up to the terms of the Enders deed and restore the park to an acceptable condition. Meanwhile, the Park and Forest Commission should stand shame-faced, with hat-in-hand, over the ruin of Enders State Forest.

THE VALLEY and SURROUNDING TOWNS

Hartfordland

The "History of Hartland," written by Stanley A. Ransom, reveals that this was the original name for the town of Hartland.

Way back on January 26, 1686, the General Court of the Colony of Connecticut gave the towns of Hartford and Windsor a grant of land in what was referred to as the "Western Lands."

Coincidentally, three months later, England sent Sir Edmund Andros to Boston as Governor of the Dominion of New England. He traveled to Hartford with armed troops seeking to secure and destroy Connecticut's Charter, which was no longer recognized by the Crown. His journey terminated at a candlelit meeting still referred to as the Charter Oak episode of October 1687. The charter, removed from the table when the room suddenly went dark, was spirited away and hidden in an ancient oak tree on the Wyllys estate. Charter intact, the Colony of Connecticut started to rule itself.

The act started a bitter controversy between the Colony and the towns of Hartford and Windsor over ownership of the Western Lands. The dispute caused problems until, in 1724, the General Court intervened and formed a committee to arbitrate the matter. A resolution was adopted as follows.

"Hartford and Windsor were given the eastern portion which now comprises the area occupied by the towns of Hartland, Colebrook, Barkhamsted, Winchester, Torrington, New Hartford and Harwinton, estimated at that time to contain about 291,806 acres. The Colony was to have the western portion containing the area occupied by the present towns of Norfolk, Goshen, North Canaan, Cornwall, Warren, and two-thirds of Kent."

On February 11, 1732, Hartford and Windsor made another division and Hartford ended up with what is now Hartland, Winchester and New Hartford.

In 1732, it was agreed the Hartland tract be divided among the proprietors of Hartford whose names appeared on the Hartford Tax List of 1720. Each man received land in proportion to the amount of tax he had paid according to Hartford's Grand List for that year. In May 1733, the General Court decreed the tract of land would be called Hartfordland. This was soon changed to Hartland.

Three villages, East Mountain, Hartland Hollow and West Mountain comprised the town. However, community activities centered in Hartland Hollow where a town hall was built.

At the north end of Hartland Hollow, Hubbard Brook flowed in from Massachusetts. It is from this point that the East Branch of the Farmington River starts. The section was actively settled, houses constructed and a school set up. Businesses opened, and it was here during the Revolutionary War that Titus Hayes started a gristmill and was officially appointed to supply grain to the Continental Army.

In 1796, Thomas Burnham built the original Red Lion Inn in Hartland Hollow. Burnham moved on prior to the Civil War. After many changes in ownership, the old inn was sold on October 25, 1911, to the Old Newgate Coon Club. It, in turn, was sold to the Metropolitan District Commission in January of 1937, and the coon club moved to its present location in Norfolk.

It became evident during the 1920s that the city of Hartford needed to plan for its future water supply to satisfy anticipated growth. The Metropolitan District Commission was formed and given the responsibility of developing reservoirs. In 1929, a bill for the construction of a dam at Barkhamsted was presented to the General Assembly. After much haggling, the East Branch Water Supply Act was passed and became law on May 14, 1931.

Things moved rapidly, and it became obvious that the water held behind the new dam would flood Hartland Hollow. The Metropolitan District purchased all the land and buildings in the village. Families left the old homesteads and the structures were razed. Generations of Hartland families lying in Hartland Hollow cemeteries were disinterred and buried again in West and East Hartland. By 1940 the Hollow had filled with water and, to this day, visitors to the area have no idea that generations lived out their lives under what is now the Barkhamsted Reservoir.

This ancient Hayes Grist Mill grinding stone in the East Hartland Cemetery commemorates the village of Hartland Hollow that was flooded to create the Barkhamsted Reservoir. Chris Levandowski photo

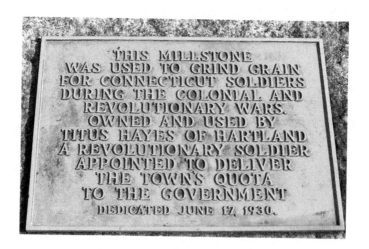

The bronze plaque on the Hayes Mill stone. Chris Levandowski photo

A piece of the old history lies in the East Hartland Cemetery. A large old millstone used by Titus Hayes reclines there with a plaque identifying its role in the life and demise of Hartland Hollow.

Axes don't cut it anymore

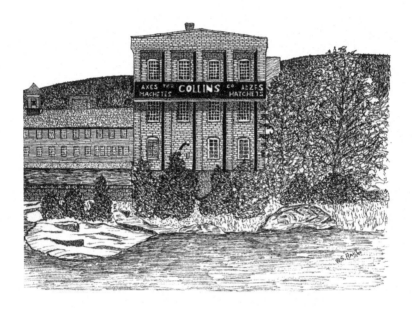

The main building of the Collins Company in Collinsville.
Pen & ink drawing by W. S. Hart

I recently had some tree work done and watched the operation with interest. The brisk activity played out amidst the cacophony created by various sized chain saws. It struck me that I didn't see anyone using an axe.

In my youth an axe was used for many tasks. The Sunday chicken met its demise with one. Fence posts were cut and driven in place with an axe. An axe split cakes of ice into manageable squares. An axe chopped stove wood and split kindling.

Throughout the years, the Collins Company in the Collinsville section of Canton was the world's dominant axe manufacturer. This small section of Canton was, until the town's incorporation in 1806, a part of the town of Simsbury. In 1826, members of the Collins family bought the Humphrey Gristmill, its water privileges and a few acres of land on the east side of the Farmington River and started the company.

Until that time, axes were crudely shaped from poor quality steel by local blacksmiths. The Collins Company grew slowly at first, however, their new mass-production methods of axe making were accepted, and the company became known worldwide for its well-balanced, keen-edged, laborsaving tools.

The new company changed manufacturing history with special furnaces spurred on by large cylinder bellows that created a high draft. In its forging shops, massive drop hammers shaped the red hot steel and used a special heat treating process to ensure that every axe maintained a sharp cutting edge long after the grinding process was complete.

Early axes were similar to the old woodshed axe we're all familiar with. As the years went by, a variety of axe heads were introduced. Loggers used a double bitted, or two-edge axe. A broad axe, with an offset handle to protect the wrist, was used to hew round logs into a square beams. To make that job easier, a smaller scoring axe cut rings around the log, at eight- to ten-inch intervals, to the depth of the required beam. The broad axe removed these smaller sections on all four sides to finish squaring off the beam.

Beams were joined with a mortise and tenon. A mortise axe and wooden maul were used to chisel a tenon (projection) on one end of the beam that fit into a mortise hole to create a strong, ninety-degree joint between two timbers. The joint was held together with a wooden treenail or "trunnel," which was shaped with a hatchet-type axe. We all recognize the typical fireman's axe.

Time went by, and the Collins Company expanded to make machetes that were in great demand for cutting sugar cane in South America. It also manufactured an extensive line of hatchets and developed a variety of adzes.

The adze is a hatchet-type implement. It is different from an axe in that its arching blade is set at a right angle to the handle. The carpenter's adze had a flat surface on the arching blade. Adzes used by ship carpenters, coopers and canoe builders had blade shapes designed for the work they had to perform.

The code of ethics of the founders of the Collins Company is interesting by today's standards. In 1827, when the first permanent buildings were erected, Sam Collins wrote in his diary: "two black men, brothers, named Quincy quarried all the stone and laid our foundations and heavy stone walls for several years. They employed a stout gang of good steady black men. The stone buildings above foundations were laid by two white masons from Hartford, Gurley and Kelly."

The foregoing paragraph seems to indicate a fair mindedness. However, looking further, his diary mentions an 1832 letter written to his employees concerning a wage dispute. He commented on their characters and said: "I am personally peculiarly gratified as it confirms me in the policy I have always adopted and advocated, viz; to employ no foreigners; none but Americans, believing them to be not only more ingenious and industrious than foreigners, but more enlightened and consequently more rational and reasonable."

Paralleling this narrow outlook, the Collins family also abided by temperance principles. To further this belief, in 1836 they built a church. The diaries also note that they "bought the old Case Tavern standing near the river and the Case farm east of the tavern, since mostly covered with houses. Purchase of the tavern was desirable to suppress gambling and drinking and to enable us to raise our dam and pond the following year."

The acquisition of the tavern backs up values Sam Collins expressed in his 1833 letter to his employees: "Instead of such disorderly and disgraceful conduct as we hear of in manufacturing communities in other countries on similar occasions and which has prejudiced some against manufacturing in this country, and to question the policy and expediency of allowing them the rights of free men at the polls, we find them here assembling quietly by the hundreds. Not at a tavern to heat their blood and warp their judgment with grog, but in the cool open air in front of the temperance store where pen and ink and paper can be procured and business conducted in a truly Republican town meeting style."

In 1833 Sam Collins summed up the problems of The Collins Company by saying:

"As there were but few axe makers in the country, we were obliged to take common blacksmiths and teach them to make axes, as they would utterly spoil some of the iron and steel and make a large quantity of poor work that could not receive our stamp and must be sold cheap, we bound them to work for several years paying but once a year and then retaining a part of their wage until an equal amount was earned on the following year. We had no difficulty in finding men to sign the contracts. Usually $14 and board the 1st year, $16 the 2nd year, $18 the third year, $20 the fourth year, $26 the fifth year, though some of the contracts were only for three years.

"The trouble with them arose after they had got to be good workmen and could get high wages elsewhere. Some ran off, forfeiting their wages. To obviate this we gave piecework by which all who could make good work got good wages, but we lost money on the inferior work done by new hands. It was only our rigid inspection and putting our name onto none but good work that enabled the establishment to survive all the vicissitudes encountered. "

During the early years, wood was the main furnace fuel. Soon charcoal, with its higher heat value, came into use and later coal became the common manufacturing fuel. Coal came up the Farmington Canal on barges to Avon and was hauled by wagon to Collinsville.

The nation and its industries grew rapidly during the late 1800s and that spurred the expansion of the railroads. The axe business became so important that, in 1850, the Canal Railroad, built on the towpath of the old Farmington Canal, and that later became the New York, New Haven & Hartford Railroad—built a branch track between Farmington and Plainville that ran northwest to Collinsville.

The track crossed the Farmington River on an iron span bridge just south of the Collins Company. The track went through the factory complex allowing direct delivery of tons of coal. Later, in 1870, it crossed the river on the north side of the complex and continued on to service factories in New Hartford.

In 1871 the Connecticut Western Railroad, which later became the Central New England Railroad, laid tracks from Hartford to Millerton, New York then ran south to Poughkeepsie, and crossed the Hudson River to connect with the western railroads at Campbell Hall, New York. In Canton, "wye" switches were installed at the High Street Junctions about a mile north of the Collins Company and a Collinsville spur was added. Heading west, trains passed the wye switches, stopped and backed into the Collinsville Station.

For those who are not railroad buffs, switches are short, moveable sections of track that direct a train from one set of tracks to another. Controlled remotely or engaged by hand, switches are turned to direct the train onto a spur, a turnout or another mainline track. A track configuration that resembles the letter "Y" is referred to as a wye switch. Wyes are installed where trains travel at very low speeds such as a railroad yard or where space is tight.

The south iron bridge remains intact. Only stone piers in the river mark the north bridge. Contrary to some opinions, the north bridge did not go out with the flood of 1955. It was dismantled when the line was discontinued.

In 1828 enterprising Collins management contracted with Oliver Couch to drive his four-horse team and stage off the Albany Turnpike (Route 44 from Hartford to Albany, New York), past its factory and through Farmington to Hartford. This change in the postal route enabled establishment of a Post Office in the village of South Canton, which soon became Collinsville.

As was true of many manufacturing communities with only one industry, the company controlled the area whether residents liked it or not. Certainly, the bank made no serious commitments without testing the approval of the Collins Company. The community's religious and educational values were strongly influenced by the morals of the Collins family.

Sons followed their fathers into the factory. Through the years, men from the hill towns of Massachusetts traveled south to the Collins Company for employment rather than endure the hardships of the farm.

The company owned the bulk of the land in the center of the village and erected buildings and sold or leased them to businesses it preferred. That rigid control prevailed until the turn of the century.

By 1832 the industry had again expanded to meet the increased demand for its excellent products. To house a growing number of employees, the company built double-occupancy houses along both sides of the river; all of a size with a simple floor plan. Their history is unique. Most still stand, only one was consumed by fire, one was torn down and a few were moved to new locations. Reports say there were some 190 company-owned houses in town.

The houses, considered unattractive by many, originally consisted of a main kitchen area, pantry, living room and one bedroom on the first floor with two sleeping rooms and a small hall above. Each house cost $500 to build, and tenants were required to take in a boarder or two. At first, the houses rented for $25 dollars a year. Board was set at $1.50 a week.

The houses are now privately owned and additions have made them more livable. Some 180 years later, they sell for prices ranging up from $149,000.

An 1869 Collinsville map shows a Samuel Collins house just north of town and across the river on a knoll, an ideal location for a factory owner to build on because it overlooked the entire factory complex. The home burned in 1912.

The Collins Company rode the crest of prosperity for 140 years. When changing times brought problems to all industries, Collins was not spared. Modern cutting tools such as chain saws, lathes, routers and shapers took the place of axes and adzes. Only the machete business continued to prosper, and the company built plants in Mexico City and Sao Paulo, Brazil, to serve those markets more competitively.

The flood of 1955 caused considerable havoc to the Collins complex; however, it was not a crushing blow. Some buildings were lost, but manufacturing continued for eleven years before the company closed its doors. Today, about half of the original fifty-plus buildings remain and house a variety of businesses, antique outlets, gift shops, art galleries and restaurants. The Canton Historical Society is located there, and that section of Collinsville is a Historic District. A bike and hiking trail built over the old railroad bed connects the complex to a network of trails and other parts of the historic town.

Even today, I can stand in the center of Collinsville and return to the Depression Days of the 1930s. I again hear the trains puffing into the station and the loud steam whistle that marked the beginning and end of every workday. The ghostly sound of trip hammers shaping hot steel, and the smell of coal smoke in the breeze make the old factory come alive once more.

The tarnished jewel

I haven't been to Hartford for over twenty years. That's a long time, but there's not much of interest any longer. This seems to be the consensus among my acquaintances except those who work there, or others who make an occasional trip to attend a function at the Wadsworth Athenaeum, The Bushnell, Hartford Stage or the Civic Center. My interest began to wane in 1945 at the end of World War II.

Plans for I-91 were in the works as early as 1940, and in 1948 construction began and sections opened as completed. In 1965 the final leg of Connecticut's 58-mile stretch of the interstate opened. Between 1948 and 1954 the original I-84 was built, and in the 1970s and 1980s it underwent major reconstruction. These routes forever changed access to downtown Hartford. Meanwhile, post-war suburbs boomed and malls sprang up. Hartford's department stores opened branches in the new malls and eventually closed their Hartford flagship stores. Restaurants and smaller retail outlets folded. The wonderful old movie theaters, already taking a hit from television, followed suit.

The stalwart old-line insurance companies like Aetna and Hartford Steam Boiler are no longer locally owned. Connecticut General (CIGNA) moved its corporate office to Bloomfield in 1957, and The Travelers has relocated some of its offices to Simsbury.

Heublien, Underwood, Royal, Silex, Arrow-Hart and Hegeman and Hartford Empire, which once held prideful positions in their industries, are gone.

At the time of Pearl Harbor (December 7, 1941), bus service had almost entirely replaced Hartford's trolleys. I took my last trolley ride about a year later.

I had enlisted and was waiting to be called to duty in the U.S. Army Air Corps. I didn't have a car, but I was dating a girl who lived in Windsor. Our dates started when I climbed on a bus from West Hartford to the Isle of Safety by the Old State House. I walked a hundred feet west to Main Street, hopped a trolley to Windsor and walked about a mile up Poquonock Avenue to her home. We walked back to Windsor center to a theater by the railroad tracks. Passing trains shook the building and drowned out the movie's soundtrack. After the show, I retraced my route back to West Hartford. It must not have been true love, because some years later I stood up as best man when she married my buddy.

Hartford was a shopping and business mecca for decades. My mother was born in 1890, and she recalled what a treat it was in 1910, to hitch up the buggy at the homestead in North Granby and head for the city. The family rode to Tariffville where they left the horse in a livery and boarded a Central New England Railroad train for Union Station in Hartford. They spent the day shopping and had a meal at the Honiss Oyster House. They often crossed State Street and attended a play at Parson's Theater; an old wooden structure that stood where the boat building is today.

Time went by, and in the 1930s several great stores competed for business and had polite clerks who actually carried on a conversation with you. Wahs Brothers, Lux Bond and Green, Gallup and Alfred, Stevens Jewelers, Clapp and Treat, Savitt Jewelers, Sisson Drug, Moyer Galleries, Stoughton Drug, Donchian's, Plimpton's, Shoor Brothers, Witkower's, Alling Rubber, Tillman's Cutlery, Florsheim, Simons Shoes, G.Fox and Company, Brown Thompson's, Sage-Allen & Co., Albert Steigers and Wise-Smith Co. In the 1930s women went to Hartford wearing dresses, hats, high-heeled shoes, and often they wore white gloves. They had luncheon in G. Fox's Connecticut Room where daily fashion shows added to the restaurant's popularity.

As a youth I couldn't afford those fancy places. I shopped at the five and dime stores: McClellans, Kresge's, 31, Woolworths, and W. T.Grant. I dined on steamed hot dogs and cold root beer at the lunch counter. If I wanted to buy sheet music, a woman played it on the piano first. I listened to a phonograph record in a soundproof booth before I bought it.

In the late 1920s Hartford was on the vaudeville circuit that went from city to city with six- or seven-act shows featuring both animals and humans. Comedians like Bob Hope, Eddie Cantor, Ed Wynn, Milton Berle, Fred Allen and Jack Benny came to Hartford.

Talking pictures that were wholesome and appealed to family audiences doomed vaudeville. When "Gone With The Wind" was released in 1939 the Motion Picture Association of America headed by Will Hays, and sometimes called the Hays office, gave special permission for Clark Gable's famous line—"Frankly my dear, I don't give a damn."—to be left in the final release.

Movie theaters, some with grand decors, seemed to be around every corner. One could choose from the Allen, Strand, Capitol, E. M. Loews, Colonial, Loews Poli Palace, Webster or Proven Pictures. Every theater had a midnight special on New Year's Eve.

Most people had favorite restaurants where the menu offered meals at reasonable prices in those Depression years. Popular eateries were the Capitol Grill, the Honiss Oyster House, Brass Rail, Spaghetti Palace, Frank's, Kid Kaplan's, City Club, Lobster House, Empire Grill, Haufbrau House, Marble Pillar, Ryan's, Round Table, Scoler's, Aetna Diner. Chicken Coop, Washington Diner, Toddle House, White Tower, Mark Twain Diner, Maple Diner, Depasquales, Heublien's, the Bond Hotel and The Hearthstone.

A popular after-dinner destination, the State Theater drew all the name bands of the times. One night I saw Tommy Dorsey and his new young singer—Frank Sinatra. "Frankie" was a skinny kid in a powder blue sport coat with padded shoulders, his hair was slicked back, and he wore pancake make-up—but how that guy could sing. I completely wore out one of his records called "I'll Never Smile Again" when I broke up with a high school sweetheart.

The annual new car show at the State Armory was among Hartford's big events. It featured all the latest models parked on plush rugs and surrounded by greenery, glittering lights and pleasing background music. Some manufacturers cut away the engine blocks and chrome plated the parts that moved up and down to show how the crankshaft, piston and valves worked. You might see a demonstration of "knee-action" or a "pushbutton" radio. Smiling salesmen stood by to pitch the new vehicles' finer qualities.

Local dealers representing all the popular manufacturers had booths. Firms such as Hartford Buick, Packard of Hartford, Gengras. Clayton Motors, Sloate Chevrolet, Grody Chevrolet, Capitol Motors, A.C. Hine Pontiac, Taber Cadillac. Neilson Ford, Eddy Nash-Lafayette, Lipman Motors, Harrington-Palmer, Beaman-Griffin, W. Hart Buick, Colonial Motors.

Hartford had a well-maintained park system and the parks were safe. Inner city residents walked to neighborhood parks where women enjoyed each other's company while their children played, old timers whiled away the hours, and everyone enjoyed band concerts in the evening.

I often mentally retrace my steps through parks named Elizabeth, Bushnell, Keeney, Pope, Goodwin, Colt's, and particularly Charter Oak that held trotting races. Bushnell Park had a huge band shell that held a full orchestra. In 1936 I saw President Franklin D. Roosevelt sitting in the back seat of an open touring car that was driven onto the stage. With a big smile and a microphone, FDR addressed the thousands standing there. Schools closed for the day so that parents could take their kids to see him in person.

Through the years, presidents and presidential candidates made stops in Hartford. I saw Wendell Willkie, Alf Landon, Dwight Eisenhower and Richard Nixon. Before television sound bites, it was a thrill to hear their rousing speeches and observe their mannerisms.

The biggest events that occurred in Hartford in my lifetime were the construction of dikes in the city's north meadows, and burying the Park River under Bushnell Park to contain and direct it to the Connecticut River.

The meadows flooded each spring when snowmelt from upper New England caused the Connecticut to overflow its banks. High water backed into the Park River where low-lying streets became canals and Bushnell Park became a lake. The band shell floated like a boat. The first floors of the telephone company, the YMCA and the Bond Hotel were inundated. Every year the Hartford *Times* and the *Courant* printed pictures of someone standing in rowboat while signing the hotel register.

When the power plant on the river was under water, electricity went out for miles around. Our family had the only gas stove on the block, so neighbors were assigned times when they could use it to cook their meals.

After the catastrophic flood of 1936 and major flooding from the Hurricane of 1938, the city asked the Army Corps of Engineers for help. In 1940 construction began on a huge concrete conduit to take the Park River underground. The Bushnell Park section was completed in 1949. Ultimately, the project spanned four decades. Today, the river goes underground near the University of Hartford, flows under the park, Pulaski Circle, the public library and Main Street before flowing into the Connecticut. The North Meadow dikes that separate the city from its original riverfront were built at about that time.

From the appearance of many men in today's work force, casual clothes seem to be the norm. In the 1940s and 1950s most of us wore a suit or a sport coat with a tie. When I started with the Travelers I had a brush-cut, and was told to let my hair grow, buy a suit and wear a hat. There were no casual Fridays. Men had pride in their clothing and supported stores such as Kennedy's, Henry Miller, Bond Clothes, Hicky-Freeman, Horsfalls, Freeman-Church, and Stackpole, Moore & Tryon.

There were shoeshine parlors, and kids with small boxes that held polish and a brush slung over their shoulders with a leather strap. If you wanted a shine, they dropped to their knees and put your foot on the top of the box and worked away.

At the parlors you could get your felt hat cleaned and steam blocked while your shoes were shined. The real dudes got a manicure at the barbershop while their hair was being cut. In those days, it was sometimes said of a salesman, "he's riding on a shoeshine and a smile."

In the late 1920s there was a steamboat landing at the foot of State Street. One big vessel that sailed from there stopped at Middletown and Saybrook before continuing on to New York City. Those excursion boats are gone, as are the steam trains that puffed into Union Station and shook the whole platform. As it waited for passengers to board, the train belched white steam and a conductor shouted, "All aboard."

The magnificent elm trees that shaded the city streets have long-since died of Dutch elm disease. Without horses, there is no need for street sweepers wearing white uniforms with heavy push brooms, shovels and barrels on wheels.

A few newspaper and magazine stands stood on the corners. In winter, men with small hand-pulled wagons sold steamed chestnuts. In summer, vendors sold popcorn with melted butter and a sprinkle of salt on top from glass-sided carts with big spoke wheels.

Christmas in Hartford was a delight. Especially G. Fox & Company with its imaginative window displays, a snow-bound Connecticut village replica on the marquee over the front doors, and a fantastic toy department where Lionel and American Flyer model trains disappeared into mountain tunnels, raced over trestles and through switchyards.

Young girls were drawn to the displays of dollhouses and the furniture to decorate them, and dolls whose eyelids closed when put down to sleep. Kids wandered around the store's tenth floor in a state of constant wonder. All year long we anticipated the trip to Fox's to sit on Santa's lap—up close to that white beard—to stutter out what we hoped to find under the tree.

Hartford was a shining jewel. It's too bad that those days are just a memory for a very few.

I thought you knew

The other day, while having tires put on at a place by the Farmington River in Farmington, I chatted with the manager who appeared to be in his early forties. The river was running high, and I mentioned that if this were the 1955 Flood, we'd be standing in waist deep water. He replied, "What's the 1955 Flood?" It dawned on me that he wasn't even born then.

This gave me pause, and I thought of some of the natural disasters that had occurred in my lifetime.

In the early spring when the snows melted up north, it was common for the Connecticut River to overflow its banks and flood vast sections of Springfield and Hartford. In 1936, after a winter of heavy snow, the flood was huge. In its aftermath dikes were built around the city and the problem was mostly solved.

Spring floods engulfed the power plant by the Connecticut River and caused power outages over a large area. In our small neighborhood in West Hartford, we were one of the few homes with a gas stove. The neighbors signed up on a posted list to reserve an hour to cook a hot meal for their families. Many of the neighbors still had old-fashioned ice boxes so some perishable foods were saved unless the power stayed off too long.

On September 21, 1938, New England was struck by a huge hurricane that came across Long Island Sound and devastated the Connecticut and Rhode Island shorelines. The storm, with winds up to186 miles per hour, roared up the Connecticut River Valley to Vermont and New Hampshire, destroying trees and property in its wake.

For a week before the storm, heavy rain fell across most of New England saturating the earth. When the winds came, the trees didn't snap off. The wind pushed them over and pulled the roots out of the ground.

Much of the property damage came from trees falling onto vehicles and structures.

At the shoreline, the catastrophe was magnified by high winds that destroyed fragile structures, and a thirty-foot tidal wave that in some areas swept everything in its path a mile inland. Beachfront cottages were swept away and smashed to kindling. Boats of all sizes ripped from their moorings and were destroyed and carried out to sea.

No early warning system existed and weather forecasting was primitive. With no prior warning of the oncoming storm, some seven hundred people were killed without a chance to flee.

In New England millions of trees were downed and it was estimated that some two million marketable trees were destroyed. Without power saws, forklifts or pay loaders the cleanup was slow. Manpower did it all with axes, two-man crosscut saws and brute strength to load the debris onto trucks.

In Providence, Rhode Island, the center of the city, built on filled marshlands, was covered with up to six feet of water in some areas. Looters came out in droves, broke plate glass windows and carried away anything they could lift.

Over the years, the disaster lay lodged deep in our memories. But, it lay dormant until August 19,1955, when the flood of the century struck Central New England.

As in 1938, its victims had no warning of the horror to come. Again rain, over several weeks, brought the water table right to the surface so the land could absorb no more moisture. A hurricane named Diane blew itself out with no major damage, but just north of its path in the Berkshires there was torrential rain.

Over thirty-six hours up to nineteen inches of rain fell and since it couldn't be absorbed, it ran into any little stream it could find and then into the Housatonic, Naugatuck and Farmington Rivers. In some areas a thirty-foot-high surge converged on cities and towns built along the rivers. Factories, commercial properties and residential areas were crushed and carried away. Roads, covered with several feet of silt, rocks and debris from upstream, remained closed for days. Entire sections of some towns remained inaccessible for weeks or even months because the raging floodwaters ripped away entire sections of roadbed and or demolished bridges.

Looking north on Rt. 189 near Silver Street and Godard Road a few days after the flood of 1955. Several feet of mud had been cleared, but not all of the debris. W. S. Hart photo

Looking south at Rt. 189 and Silver Street after the 1955 flood that washed the old Cragg Mill from its foundations. W. S. Hart photo

Damages were estimated at over a billion dollars in real dollars, not the inflated dollars of today. Over thirty thousand people were left homeless, some one hundred died and four thousand were injured. The job loss was never fully estimated, but it was severe. Towns recovered, but many never looked the way they had before that September day.

DO YOU REMEMBER?

Being a Connecticut Yankee

When you get through reading this, I'm sure many of you are going to think of me as a cheapskate, a miser, a skinflint or a penny pincher, but back when I was a kid "Connecticut Yankee" meant being a sharp trader, playing your cards close to the vest and being penurious.

Some of that rubbed off on me. When I look back to the 1930s, I remember driving a small delivery truck for twenty-five cents an hour. A forty-hour week netted me ten dollars. Working ten hours a day, six days a week for a total of sixty hours was the way to earn overtime, which was only paid after you put in sixty hours.

Senior citizens always regale us with stories of how inexpensive things were in the old days. For a quarter one could get a haircut, go to a movie, get three tokens to ride the bus or trolley or even buy a pack of cigarettes.

Even a nickel was a big deal. It bought a cup of coffee and a doughnut, an ice cream cone, gum, lifesavers, a Baby Ruth candy bar. A pay telephone cost a nickel, as did playing a song on a jukebox or playing a pinball machine. Even the tooth fairy paid five cents for a tooth under the pillow. The best buy was penny candy. A Roosevelt dime was good for a sandwich, a hot dog or even a piece of pie. Wealthier people, those who made more than twenty-five cents an hour, ordered the blue plate special at a fine restaurant for a $1.25.

When I was discharged from the Air Force in 1945, I worked for the Aetna Life Insurance Company for $25 a week. Today, grade school kids get more than that for an allowance. Enough of that old stuff. Times have changed and I have to adjust to it even though it's difficult.

Paying over $3.50 a gallon for gas and even more for heating fuel scares me. I get a tight feeling when I check out at the local Stop & Shop. A few items cost more than I made a week when I was earning $3,000 a year in 1950.

It really hit home when my daughter and son-in-law gave my lady companion and me a $100 gift certificate to a restaurant in Farmington. Not being big eaters, we figured if we had a modest dinner, we could save the balance of the gift for lunch another day. Our plans were shattered when the check arrived—$98! With a twenty-percent tip, that was almost $120. You can imagine what that did to this old Yankee.

Today's incomes far exceed those of my generation. Some young families live in houses with a three-car garage that cost in the range of $750,000. Some also have a time-share condominium at a posh resort area.

I did some figuring. Young people still on the way up are making more in a week that I did in a month at the height of my career. I bought my first house in 1959 and paid $17,000 for it. In 1980 I bought a new car for the same amount of money.

My modest pension is based on the low salaries of years ago. The big problem for us oldies is that the cost of the necessities of life is geared to today's high incomes. A haircut at the senior's rate is $15. Since my income doesn't go up, I don't even leave a tip anymore.

I shouldn't be a crybaby. I have a good life. I'm on borrowed time; life expectancy tables say I should have died eight years ago at age seventy-nine. I have no regrets. In fact, I've had the words "He lived," engraved on my marker that's waiting for a final date to be put on it in the family plot.

This old bird is glad his ties go back to those cantankerous Connecticut Yankees.

"As you are now so once was I"

When I was a young man I saw the above epitaph engraved on a cemetery marker where an elderly man was buried. I was struck with his sentiment, and suddenly realized that he too had lived and experienced the joys and sorrows of his generation as well as a deep love for one also now departed.

In my senior years, I think of that expression, and hope my grandchildren pause to wonder if I had an interesting youth somewhat different from theirs.

They can't parallel my memories because they have no idea of what a cistern is, how to prime the water pump in the kitchen sink or trim the wick on a kerosene lantern.

My grandchildren missed driving a team of horses and feeling the tug of a pair of reins. They can't recall the snort of a horse or the metal clang of its iron shoe hitting a rock.

They won't ever sit on a handmade wooden stool to milk a cow. They won't know the warmth of her hide, or those moon eyes that quietly looked at you as she patiently chewed her cud. It took a few hand pulls before the cow "let-down" and milk squirted freely into the pail. I could describe it to them, but they will never know the tightness that came to my forearms after milking a few cows. My uncle and I milked twenty head morning and night so the muscles hurt frequently.

Chances are they'll never see a farmer riding a mowing machine pulled by a team, or watch him occasionally push the foot lever to raise the cutting bar over a rock or other obstruction. Not many remember the clicking of the wheel ratchet as the mower was backed up.

I don't even have a picture of a one-horse hay rake making windrows in the field to show them. With modern hay balers, gone is the sight of a man using a pitchfork to roll the windrows into haycocks. They'll never be startled as I was atop the wagon full of hay when my uncle playfully tossed a black snake up to me. I dodged, and was ready to leap from the wagon when I realized the snake was dead and decapitated by the mowing machine. It was great to lie on my back on the springy, sweet smelling hay as the team pulled the loaded wagon up the dirt road to the barn.

I still get a good feeling when I recall the first time my uncle let me back the team and wagon up to the haymow.

Even if my grandchildren cut the grass, they have no idea of the feel or the sound of a well-oiled hand lawnmower. If they clear leaves, it is with a leaf blower instead of a hand rake, and that long driveway is easier cleared with a snow blower than a shovel.

It's wonderful to live in a warm house without supplying the heat by going to the wood lot with an axe, cutting the trees down, and hauling them to the woodshed where they were cut up and split to stove and furnace lengths.

Warm showers are refreshing, but a long way from having to pump the water, heat it on the stove and pour it into a circular galvanized tub.

Can they understand the aching tiredness in my arms and back from picking up the harvested corn stalks to load them on a wagon, and tossing them down to the ensilage cutter that blew it up into the silo?

They don't know the exhilaration of standing on the narrow top step of an orchard ladder to pick apples from the top of the tree. They'll also miss making their own cider and maybe getting a buzz when it turned hard.

Grandchildren, you've missed the quiet warmth of a cow barn in winter, and the disturbed clucking of a hen when you reached under her to find the warm eggs.

How sad to have missed the awe of walking a snow-covered cow pasture following animal tracks, and suddenly seeing the ever-present turkey vulture quietly floating overhead looking for carrion.

So many things young people do today were foreign to my youth because we waited until we were adults to experience them. Magazines in the convenience store don't leave much to the imagination. My buddies and I learned something of the female form by sneaking peeks at the corset ads in the Sears Roebuck catalog or photos in the National Geographic Magazine.

It sure would be corny for these kids to bob for apples, play post office, spin the bottle or pull taffy!

The lost sounds of yesteryear

The other night I was thinking of the quieter days of my childhood in the 1930s on my grandfather's farm in North Granby. There was no electricity—we had no radio, and television hadn't been invented yet.

The only man-made intrusion was an infrequent party-line telephone call. By counting the rings, we could tell who was being called.

In summer, the entire family sat on the front porch in wooden rocking chairs. In the darkness we listened to sounds of the countryside. With the exception of some small talk, we found peace in contemplating our own thoughts.

If there was no breeze, we heard the water running over the big dam at the crag a quarter of a mile away. If it was very calm we could make out the voices of people talking by the millpond.

Just at dusk, on a clear night, we watched slim, speedy nighthawks wheeling and swooping after insects. As twilight fell we listened to the soft clucking from the chicken house as the hens settled on their roosts.

Most roads were dirt, and few cars ventured out at night. Sometimes we'd hear and see the dim yellowish headlights of a car going up the road. Often, by the sound of the motor, we identified the car as belonging to Harry Day or another farmer in the area.

On hot August evenings we watched the blinking fireflies and listened to the "knee-deep, knee-deep" from the frog pond accompanied by a chorus of high-pitched katydid songs.

My father smoked a pipe, and the frequent scratch and quick flare of a blue-tip match accompanied his relighting of the pipe. There was a hot, sizzling sound as he drew on the pipe stem, and drifting smoke helped keep the stinging mosquitoes away.

Looking back I often wonder why our two work horses pawed the plank floors of their stalls and whinnied a couple of times before settling in for the night.

In the house, we turned up the kerosene lamps and sat around the dining room table. The lamps weren't great to read by or to look at catalogs, but it was better than candles. There was almost complete silence unless someone wanted a glass of water. He or she worked the handle up and down on the pump in the kitchen sink, and I still hear the sound of water gushing and splashing into the glass. That silvery water was clear and cold.

After retiring for the night, lying there in the double bed was deathly quiet unless a breeze stirred the leaves. High winds shook the old mortise-and-tenon house and blew around the sharp corners of the eaves, which caused a whistling effect.

During a loud thunderstorm, a flash of lightning lit the room like daytime. I counted the seconds until I heard the clap of thunder to determine how many miles away it had struck. I remember, in one violent storm, hearing a tree go down in the pasture on the mountainside.

When dawn came, the lifter on the stove lid clanged as I removed it to poke the banked ashes and crank the grates before adding split firewood to the iron stove.

Walking the path to the cow barn in the glistening dew, I noticed the mist rising from the small brook and heard the gurgle and splash as the water flowed around shiny, moss-covered rocks.

When the cows ambled through the big barn door, their hooves clop-clopped on the cement floor. With a "clatch" noise, each cow was snapped into its stanchion. Each received a quart measure of grain, which was followed by the sandpaper sounds of big tongues licking it from the cement at the front of the stalls.

Then came the soft scraping of the small milk stool's wooden legs as you slid it to the proper distance for milking. The first squirts of milk into the shiny metal pail had a high, sharp, almost pinging note and became a deeper, steadier sound as the milk level rose. When the pail was almost full, the streams squirting through the froth were muffled.

With twenty cows under that low ceiling, hundreds of flies congregated, and their wings created a rising and falling symphony of incessant buzzing.

Metal drinking bowls mounted between every two stanchions were fed by water piped down from a well up on the mountain. Each had a spring-loaded metal disk at the bottom, and as the cow's nose pushed down on it, the bowl filled with water. It sounded much like a toilet tank does when it refills.

When a cow turned her head, the short chains attached to the top and bottom of her stanchion made a clacking sound.

Lest we forget—some words from our past

The other day, the words of a poem I wrote long ago came into my thoughts: "I recall when I was small, the sounds, in dead of night, of whistling, steam powered trains."

That gave me pause, and I couldn't help but think of how many words common to my youth are no longer familiar.

When I was a kid, houses weren't as tightly sealed as those of today and frequently crickets came in. It was a chore to chase down that chirping sound and throw the insect outside. This lead me to think that with today's lawn chemicals, I no longer see grasshoppers or watch a robin standing with its head cocked, searching for a worm in the moist lawn. I don't see as many fireflies either.

Have you noticed we don't hear the word "lath" used anymore. In the days of abundant tobacco growing, a four-foot-long, two-inch-wide, half-inch-thick lath was used to hang tobacco in the sheds for curing. A small, pointed-metal tip was placed on the end of a lath to spear the thick end of a tobacco stalk that had been cut off at ground level. When it held several stalks, the lath was hung, leaves down, between two long parallel rails on a wagon and drawn to the barn. There it joined many tiers of lath hung on the rafters. Shade grown tobacco used the same lath, but each leaf had been picked from the stalk, sewn on a string then strung onto the lath.

Before modern sheetrock walls, those same laths were nailed horizontally, an inch apart, on the wall studs and ceilings to hold the plaster that was troweled on by hand. The pure-white plaster was mixed at ground level at the building site. A shallow, rectangular metal tub was filled with dry plaster and water was folded in with a wide hoe. The plaster was scooped into a hod, which was a two-foot long, V-shaped wooden troth that sat atop a pole. A hod carrier rested it on his shoulder and took it to the plasterer. A similar hod was used to carry the bricks and mortar when building a chimney.

When I was young, all the kids knew what to call the two curved wood and metal pieces that attach to the sides of a draft horse's collar as part of its harness. They are "hames." Heavy leather "trace" or "tug" straps attach to the hames, pass through rings on the side of the girth strap and, at the other end, attach to the "whippletree." Trace straps transfer the horse's pull from the chest collar to the load.

Maybe you know what the "whippletree" or "whiffletree" is. It is a pivoted bar placed between the wagon pole or tongue and the traces (tugs) of a harness. It balances the pull from each side of a single horse as it moves forward, or balances the pull between two horses in a team.

When working a team of horses, the "nigh" horse is on the left. and the "off" horse on the right. Therein lies the meaning of the old expression, "He was as independent as Job's off ox." A skittish horse might be distracted by the world around it, so you blocked its side vision with small leather "blinders" attached to the bridle next to each eye, which allowed the horse to only see forward. Another old saying comes to mind—"He went through life with blinders on."

We no longer hear anyone refer to "winnowing." It means separating the wheat from the chaff. A hundred years ago, hand-cranked wooden winnowing machines did the job. At the beginning of America, the job was done by hand labor. A farmer built his barn with two large doors on opposite sides of the building so the wind blew through. The harvested wheat was put on the floor and the farmer used a hand flail to beat the grain from the stalks. When this was done, the farmer used a wide wooden shovel to toss the beaten material into the air. The wind blew the chaff away, and the grain dropped to the floor.

When a farmer started out, his first task was to build a barn to house his stock and store the feed. It might have been years before a house was built, so the family lived at one end of the barn. To get to the living area one crossed the threshing floor and that's why a doorsill is called a threshold.

Today we take the snow tire for granted, but I find its beginnings interesting. In the 1920s and 1930s car owners put chains on their tires to get through snow, which worked just fine. When spring came the snow melted, and those unpaved country roads became a huge mud problem. Farmers complained, and the tire industry invented a heavily grooved tire called a "mud" tire. Low and behold, the mud tire also worked in snow and a new industry was on its way.

The old tire chain had its day, but it was a nuisance when driving on bare pavement. The short cross-links frequently wore out. When one end of a link broke, the freed link "rap, rap, rapped" against the underside of the fender well. Some smart guy came up with "monkey links," which were short lengths that were easily clamped in place to replace a broken link.

Snubber is another vintage word from my memory book. Years ago it functioned in the same way a shock absorber does today.

Some may think this is a lot of nonsense; but hopefully some of you had fun recalling the phrases of long ago.

Fifty years from now

Fifty years from now will today's youth look back at these times as "the good old days?" The common denominators of love, marriage, birth, death, taxes, employment and God will survive, but the basic mechanics of everyday living will have changed dramatically.

Will they remember this era of noise, and air and water pollution with nostalgia? Will they recall bumper-to-bumper traffic as relaxing? Will the stench of exhaust fumes, and the cesspools our streams have become be looked back on with pride? Unfortunately, they won't have the charm and peace of 1920s and 1930s to recall for comfort. None will recall the simple pleasures of everyday life in those pre-WWII days.

They won't remember the soft stretch of the spring on a screen door, or the buzzing of flies before they were trapped by sticky flypaper. They won't think of the pleasant whir of a well-oiled, hand-pushed lawnmower or the rhythmic idle of a 1930 Model A Ford.

Right now, do you remember the clip-clop of the milkman's horse; the sound of an ice pick on a twenty-pound block of ice, the drip of melting water collecting in the pan under an old wooden ice box; the swish of a Bissell carpet sweeper; hand-beating a carpet thrown over the clothesline; anticipating the taste of ice cream while turning the crank on an ice cream churn; a rooster crowing at dawn; a sprinkling truck watering the streets; a trolley bell; the thrill of an excursion boat ride; sheet music at the five and dime; going into a booth to try a record before buying it; flag root candy; dandelion greens with vinegar; riding on the top of a load of hay; driving the one-horse hay rake; backing a wagon into a barn with a team of horses; weaning a calf to a pail; cider made from your own apples; the warm pleasant noises of a cow barn in winter; horses stomping their hooves on wooden stall floors; the smell of Flit sprayed in the barn to keep down the flies; milling by hand instead of a machine; swimming by the dam at the grist mill; splitting wood in the shed for the iron stove in the kitchen;

the soft springy ride of a buggy; cutting ice on the pond; pumping an old reed organ; singing along with a melody from a roll on the player piano; shooting off fireworks such as cherry bombs, lady fingers, three-inchers, Roman candles, pinwheels and sky rockets; Saturday matinee movie serials; free dish night; amateur night and sing-along to the rhythm of the bouncing ball at the local movie house; respect for the President; collecting bottle caps, match covers and pictures of movie stars; chopping through ice in the watering trough; cars with no heaters or radios; clapping the erasers at school; a dip pen and ink well; setting pans of fresh milk in the pantry to let the cream rise; trousers with suspender buttons; the sound of corduroy knickers; taffy pulls; spin the bottle and post office; priming a pump; a one-dollar Ingersol pocket watch with a fob; being snowed in for days and, finally, cod liver oil?

We weren't allowed to drink Coke because it was habit forming, but Moxie was all right? How about riding an open-air trolley out to the country or having a shore dinner by Long Island Sound when shellfish was native and edible?

Evenings lighted by kerosene lamps with their different colored shades. Real iced tea—made with clean water from a driven well—instead of the powdered kind.

It's foolish to think fruits and vegetables from a Mason jar tasted better than those in cans or frozen, but homemade root beer was far superior to today's commercial brands.

I'll take the memories of my youth and once again walk barefooted down a country road and feel the fine dust squish up between my toes. The brooks were clean and the trout were not liver-fed by the state fish hatchery.

The present generation is smarter than I, and will greatly surpass me in worldly goods. However, they'll never have the wholesome memories of that time in this nation's history before it changed from a rural, pastoral way of life to a city-oriented culture where most are strangers among men.

Many years ago

My lady companion and I are in our eighties, and we two old timers have fun thinking back to the past when times weren't so hectic and people had time for people. Many of you have read similar pieces but I think it is worth repeating. Back in 1987, she was asked to speak at the fiftieth reunion of her 1937 high school class in Plainville. Fortunately she kept a copy of that speech that I can share with you.

Since June of 1937 we have all seen many changes. Just think we were before computers, before the pill and the population explosion. We were before television, penicillin, polio shots, antibiotics, and Frisbees. There were no frozen foods, nylons, Dacron, Xerox or the Kinsey Report, and we hadn't yet seen radar, fluorescent lights, credit cards and ballpoint pens.

In our time, closets were for clothes not for coming out of, and a book about two women living together in Europe could be called "Our Hearts Were Young and Gay." Bunnies were small rabbits, and rabbits were not Volkswagens. We were before Grandma Moses, Frank Sinatra and cup-sizing bras. We wore Peter Pan collars and thought a deep cleavage was something the butcher did.

We were before Batman, "Grapes of Wrath," Rudolph the Red Nosed Reindeer and Snoopy. Before DDT and vitamin pills, the wine craze, disposable diapers and Jeeps. Before students took a term off, before scotch tape, the Grand Cooley Dam, M&Ms, the automatic shift and Lincoln Continentals. Before pizzas, Cheerios, frozen orange juice, instant coffee, McDonald's, Howard Johnson's and Friendly's.

We thought fast food was what you ate during Lent. We were before FM radio, tape recorders, electric typewriters, word processors, Muzak and disco dancing. We were before air travel went commercial; almost no one flew across the country and trans-Atlantic flights belonged to Lindbergh and Amelia Earhart.

We were before pantyhose, drip-dry clothes, ice makers, dishwashers, clothes dryers, freezers and electric blankets. Before students held cocktail parties on campuses and the opposite sex was allowed above the first floor. Before Hawaii and Alaska became states. Before men wore long hair and earrings and women wore slacks.

We were before Leonard Bernstein, yogurt, Ann Landers, plastics, hair dryers, the forty-hour week, minimum wage and premarital sex (it says here). Anyway we got married first and then lived together; how quaint can you be?

In our day cigarette smoking was fashionable, grass was mowed, Coke was something you drank and pot was something you cooked in. We were before day-care centers, househusbands, computer dating and dual careers. When we had a baby it was a seven-day hospital event, not something you did on the way to work. We were before coin vending machines, jet planes, helicopters, and interstate highways. "Made in Japan," meant junk and the term "making out" referred to how you did on your exam.

In our time there were five and dime stores where you could buy things for five or ten cents. For just one nickel you could ride the subway, make a phone call, buy a Coke or enough stamps to mail one letter and two postcards. You could buy a Chevy Coupe for $659, but who could afford it in 1937? A pity, because gas cost eleven cents a gallon.

If anyone, in those days, had asked us to explain CIA, NATO, UFO, NFL, SATs, JFK, BMW, ERA or IUD, we would have said alphabet soup. We were not before the difference between the sexes was discovered, but we were before sex changes; we just made do with what we had. And we were the last generation that was so dumb as to think you needed a husband to have a baby.

We wore girdles with garters and petticoats and serge bloomers for gym. We mailed our laundry home from school in cardboard boxes and it came back with brownies. We had fountain pens and bottles of real ink. We had all of the big bands: Tommy Dorsey, Glen Gray, and Guy Lombardo. Unlike remote control dancers of today, we knew how it felt to have your partner hold you close and double dip. We played thick, 78 rpm records with cactus needles that always needed sharpening. We had Toscanini, Koussevitzky, Flagstad and Edward the VIII.

We can't forget saddle shoes, loafers and convertibles with rumble seats or nights on the beach by a campfire listening to a portable Victrola as Ray Noble played "The Very Thought of You" on his piano.

Those fifty years were interesting and I'll bet even the kids of today, though reluctantly, might just think we old gray hairs did have a pretty good life.

What will I miss?

This old guy has reached the stage of life where the grim reaper is cutting into my rank of friends and family with his silent scythe; seemingly choosing at random. If there is a great beyond, and I have some awareness, I wonder what I will miss from this old earth.

Maybe it will be the sound of the Good Humor truck, Saturday matinees with never-ending serials, building a tree house, making a swing out of a rope and an old tire, Guy Lombardo on New Year's Eve, snappy vaudeville with seven or eight comedy acts, a ride on an open-air trolley with its bell clanging, ping pong, water pistols, pea shooters, sling shots,

BB guns, my father's root beer, feasting on dark purple Concord grapes and spitting out the seeds, cold watermelon on the Fourth of July, skinny dipping in a hidden brook, playing marbles, roller skating, riding a scooter, licking the frosting bowl, the first spring day when I shed corduroy knickers for short pants, trying to play hopscotch with the girls, realizing that girls were different, collecting warm eggs from under the hen as she clucked at me, feeling the soft muzzle of a horse, the clatter sounds of a horse-drawn mowing machine, the jerky tug of reins while driving a team of horses, pitching horseshoes, feeling the pull of a trout on the line, letting go of a Tarzan rope over the pond, the crisp sounds of dried leaves gathered with a bamboo rake, digging into the deep snow drift by the stoop, seeing and hearing leafless tree branches flail each other like buggy whips, the drip of sap into a tin pail, snapping fireplace logs, white wood smoke easing out of the chimney into the frigid air, the lapping of waves upon the shore, the smell of an inlet at low tide, horse hooves clopping on an old dirt road, the whistle of a steam powered train in the dead of night, the adrenalin rush of my first take-off in a Piper Cub, the crack of the ball on the bat, sounds of a cap pistol, the path of a Roman candle swooshing into the night sky, blowing smoke rings in the quiet air, the mournful sound of a fog horn, the wagging tail of a happy dog, the sounds from the frog pond, the sad call of a mourning dove, a hummingbird pestering a flower blossom, a chorus of katydids in late August, the call of a night owl, the downward scale of an evening thrush at dusk, hearing a cricket in the house in winter, the hurt from the rungs on the ladder while picking apples, pulling a radio station in on a crystal set, the sound of rain on the roof in the attic, the sound of wind-blown ice crystals hitting the frozen snow, spring peepers in the swamp, the smell of freshly plowed soil, water pouring over the dam at the millpond, a moonlight ride in a rumble seat on a starry night, the cracking sound of a tall tree just as the last axe stroke sets it free, the relaxing snort of a workhorse at the end of the day, a cow's sad eyes, the mist over a small stream at dawn, feeling the smooth mesh of gears when shifting my stick-shift Ford, sensing the bond between man and beast as I drove the team, feeling the first blush of "puppy love" on my first date in junior high school, the closeness I had with my kids when they were little, realizing there aren't any people older than I to give me sage advice, the strong sexual desires of the younger years, sitting on an upright radiator to get warm after playing in the snow, fishing with a can of worms, catching fireflies in a jar, collecting frog's eggs and watching them turn into tadpoles, scavenger hunts, breaking ice in the milk house water troth, swimming and diving without effort, holding a newborn child, running up a flight of stairs two at a time, playing the piano with nimble fingers, walking the hills without hurting knees, sleeping the night through, climbing a ladder to clean the gutters, the wind in my hair with the convertible top down, holding hands, singing in the choir, pitching hay, movies without vulgarity and violence, the Big Band Era, love for our flag, respect for politicians and authority, a woman's soft voice saying my name over candlelight, waking up to the smiles and nice words of my companion, a walk together, a glass of wine by the fireplace and recalling shared memories going back over sixty-five years.

Remember when television was great?

During the last few years, the quality of TV programs has hit the skids. With the exception of a few stations like A&E, Discovery Channel, Biography, History Channel and Public Television, I've arrived at a point where enough is enough.

The local channels' newscasts are nothing but two anchors giggling with one another, and joking with a weatherman who is mostly wrong with his forecasts.

Cable news broadcasts cover the same event over and over again. We're inundated with upcoming presidential election nonsense that nobody really cares about. Remember how they killed us with the O. J. Simpson trial and the impeachment of what's his name?

Today's situation comedies make me cringe. It appears that producers, in a quest for younger viewers, push sex, violence, foul language, disrespect for authority, wise-apple kids and stupid fathers.

I consider commercials to be an invasion of my privacy. Think about it. Becoming involved in a program it is like listening to a friend telling you a story, and suddenly some idiot breaks into the conversation with some drivel that has nothing to do with the subject matter.

I think some entrepreneur should come up with a pay-not-to-view gadget that automatically blocks a commercial the moment its increased volume comes on.

How many of you, in mixed company, want to be subjected to ads for personal hygiene products, medications for conditions that used to be considered private, sexy women's undergarments and those for the incontinent?

A wonderful media is killing itself. Fifty years ago, in its infancy, the networks knew they had something: a magnet for the masses that occasionally paid cash to see a movie. For free, right in their own living rooms (with only an occasional advertisement), they could be entertained.

A similar thing happened in the 1930s when my generation was mesmerized by the radio that pulled sound right out of the air. No more cranking up an old Victrola. My family's first radio, a Fada, ran on storage batteries. I also had a crystal set. All it required was a ground wire running to the radiator and another strung to a pole on the garage as an antenna. Inside the set, a wound copper wire, with a piece of spring called a "cat's whisker" on top, was scratched on a small metal crystal until you picked up a local radio station in the single headphone. Wow!

When radio and its varied shows came into the house, we sat in a semi-circle to listen to the words read from a script in the studio. We each interpreted the words in our own way and conjured up images that the words described. We did our own thinking rather than soaking up an image the producer throws at us.

I recall the enjoyment of those old radio shows when we tuned in for Amos and Andy, Myrt and Marge, Major Bowes Amateur Hour, Fred Allen, Eddie Cantor, Jack Armstrong the All American Boy, Tom Mix, The Lone Ranger, Little Orphan Annie, Jack Benny, Lux Radio Theater, Bell Telephone Hour, Fred Waring and his Pennsylvanians, The Shadow, Lights Out, Father Coughlin, One Man's Family, Ma Perkins, Lum and Abner, Kate Smith, Ed Wynn and the news with Lowell Thomas, H.V. Kaltenborn, and Edward R. Morrow.

One of radio's most memorable moments came on December 8, 1941, when Franklin D. Roosevelt addressed a joint session of Congress. In his first sentence he described the previous day's attack by Japan on Pearl Harbor as, "a day that will live in infamy." I still recall his famous Fireside Chats, and his saying: "my friends, I hate war and my wife Eleanor, hates war."

I was married in 1949, and we lived in a two-room, $45-a-month apartment. We brightened it up by buying a ten-inch Philco television that had rabbit ears for an antenna. We were fascinated even though the viewing hours were limited. At first, we even watched the test pattern while we waited for a show to begin. In those days shows broadcast "live" meaning it went on the air with no editing. If an actor or commentator flubbed his lines that was what we saw.

The first comedian I recall watching was Jerry Lester on Broadway Open House. His co-star was a statuesque blond named Dagmar, an early version of Dolly Parton.

Then there was Your Show of Shows with Sid Caesar and Imogene Coca. How about Arthur Godfrey and the popular singer, Julius LaRosa, whom he fired on the air? The Ed Sullivan Show and all the varied talent he introduced to the world.

Close your eyes a moment and think of:

The Untouchables, Mission Impossible, The Bob Hope Show, Jack Benny and Mary Livingston, Gary Moore, Lonesome George Gobel, Dinah Shore, Jackie Gleason, Perry Como, Flip Wilson, Smothers Brothers, Rowan and Martin, Ernie Kovacks, Steve Allen, Jack Paar, Dave Galloway, Johnny Carson, Orson Wells, Art Linkletter, Burns and Allen, Dean Martin, Franks Sinatra Show, Liberace, Tennessee Ernie Ford, Jimmy Durante, Milton Berle, Red Skelton, Ken Murray, Ted Mack, Roy Rogers and Dale Evans, Gunsmoke, Mannix, Dragnet, Kojak, The Fugitive, Mary Tyler Moore Show, Andy Griffith, Columbo, Bob Newhart, Ironsides, Danny Thomas, Fibber McGee and Molly, Have Gun Will Travel, Hawaii Five-0, Herb Shiner, Mr. Ed, Highway Patrol, Hogan's Heroes, The Honeymooners, The Jeffersons, Life of Riley, Leave It To Beaver, Life With Father, Marcus Welby, MD, Maverick, Merv Griffin Show, My Three Sons, What's My Line?, Your Hit Parade, Our Miss Brooks, Perry Mason, Peyton Place, Rawhide, The Odd Couple, Dick Van Dyke Show, Dick Cavett, The Defenders, Dr. Kildaire, Father Knows Best, McCloud, Bonanza, M.A.S.H., Laverne and Shirley, Archie Bunker, Gomer Pyle, Sergeant Bilko, Welcome Back Kotter, Dobie Gillis, Gilligan's Island, Abbott and Costello, The Waltons, Starsky and Hutch, Sunset Strip, Little House on the Prairie, and many more that don't come to mind.

Political conventions used to be interesting. Before modem day primaries, presidential and vice presidential candidates were chosen at the conventions. Speeches were oratorical and the fanfare for each native son was worth watching. From anchor booths a floor or two above the crowd, Walter Cronkite, David Brinkly and John Chancellor offered wise commentary. Reporters on the floor scurried between delegations to keep abreast of the infighting. When a vote was called, I waited to hear, loud and clear, "Alabama passes."

At the 1968 Democrat convention in Chicago, violent demonstrations broke out in the streets. From the podium, Connecticut's Senator Abraham Ribicoff called Mayor Daly's handling of the matter "Gestapo tactics" for the whole nation to see. Only those who could lip-read caught Daly's response.

The mechanics of television are great: color, zoom lenses, instant replay and in-car cameras to name a few. I have to say, however, that I feel television killed radio and is now feeding its own demise. Eventually, the public will reject the junk.

Expressions of yesteryear

I wonder whether or not any of my companion elders will agree that present day conversations may be factual, but they are not very entertaining. I miss the humor of sentences spoken fifty years ago.

Lately, the public appears to be stuck on three repetitive expressions: "basically," "ya know" and that boring word, "awesome."

What is colorful speech? The youth of today may think I'm around the bend, but as you read the following you may recall what I'm referring to or remember some I've forgotten.

Independent as a hog on ice; wrinkled as a worrier's brow; handsome is as handsome does; always darkest before the dawn; wire-to-wire; down the hatch; dead as a mackerel; out of the frying pan into the fire; a watched pot never boils; the proof is in the pudding; a bird in the hand is worth two in the bush; a penny saved is a penny earned; happy as a clam at high tide; the world is my oyster; beauty is only skin deep; any port in a storm; rich as Croesus; don't put the cart before the horse; where there's smoke there's fire; it's a long road that has no turning; raining cats and dogs; the buck stops here; don't put your neck on the block; don't cut off your nose to spite your face; age before beauty; if you dance to the tune, you have to pay the piper; chickens always come home to roost; blow your top; half baked; dead serious; never look a gift horse in the mouth; there's no place like home; it takes two to tango; there's no fool like an old fool; as scarce as hens' teeth; let sleeping dogs lie; don't buy a pig in a poke; sink or swim; there's many a slip between the cup and the lip; home is where the heart is; you can't make a silk purse out of a sow's ear; time and tide wait for no man; don't miss the boat; the grass is always greener on the other side; birds of a feather flock together; as ye sow so shall ye reap; the apple doesn't fall far from the tree; get the cow then the calf; the old college try; slippery as an eel; a close shave; like pulling teeth; clear as crystal; cold as a fish; smooth as silk; as quiet as a church mouse; sharp as a tack; dry as a bone; thin as a shadow; toe the line; free as the breeze; high as a kite; crazy as a loon; lock-stock-and-barrel; every cloud has a silver lining; it's an ill wind that doesn't blow some good; mad as a hatter; pretty as a picture; ugly as a hedge fence; sly as a fox; clam-up; toot your own horn; leap to a conclusion; smart as a whip; stubborn as a mule; wise as an owl; living on a shoe string;

on cloud nine; nose to the grindstone; eager beaver; at a snail's pace; a slip of the tongue; mend your ways; white as a sheet; pure as the driven snow; the ties that bind; wear your heart on your sleeve; heart to heart; until the cows come home; bald as a billiard ball; strong as an ox; pull your own weight; thin as a rail; barking up the wrong tree; sour grapes; behind the eight ball; straight arrow; eye to eye; flow with the current; meek as a lamb; happy as a lark; pie in the sky; green as grass; as old as the hills; don't swim upstream; true blue; nutty as a fruit cake; easy as pie; a barrel of laughs; chip off the old block; rule the roost; mad as a wet hen; cool as a cucumber; hotter than a two dollar pistol; out on a limb; black as pitch; apple of your eye; keep an ear to the ground; on your toes; put all your ducks in a row; cock of the walk; no skin off my nose; fly off the handle; stick to your guns; close shave; slick as a whistle; make hay while the sun shines; waste not want not; well-heeled; a kernel of truth; a-hop-skip-and-a-jump; sore as a pup; quick as a flash; sour apples; sweet as pie; tough nut to crack; slow as molasses; quick as a wink; sleek as a cat; tough as a board; tongue in cheek; neat as a pin; head over heels; short and sweet; a squeaky hinge gets the oil; high and dry; up to your ears; a slip of the tongue; a stitch in time saves nine; holding all the cards; tight as a tick; shadow of a doubt; sore as a boil; glimmer of hope; can't hold a candle to; up the creek; tighter than a drum; loose as a goose; paddle you own canoe; drive a hard bargain; if the shoe fits wear it; tough as toenails; stick like flypaper; jump for joy; a tongue lashing; don't drag your feet; scrape the bottom of the barrel; like the pot calling the kettle black; water seeks its own level; cream rises to the top; funny as a crutch; limp as a rag; don't put all your eggs in one basket; save for a rainy day; break a leg; you can't fly on one wing; rule the roost; count your chickens; face the music; school of hard knocks; thick as a log; on thin ice; cheap skate; fat cat; pull in your belt; follow your heart; one step at a time; until the cows come home; better late than never; deaf as a post; tight as a fiddle; flat as a pancake; blood is thicker than water; weak as a cat; pouring buckets; as fast as greased lightning; smell a rat; easy as falling off a log; dead as a doornail; mad as a wet hen; purr like a kitten; heavy as lead; light as a feather; bold as brass; a look that would sour milk; butter wouldn't melt in her mouth; a face that would stop a clock; where there's a will there's a way; hope is eternal; charity begins at home; home is where the heart is; as clear as mud; thick as thieves; rough as a cob; lies like a rug; a shot in the arm; sick as a dog; quick as a flash; warm as toast; the ties that bind; my lips are sealed; bald as an eagle; green as grass; guilty as sin; keep a stiff upper lip; the bottom line; a nose for news; thin as a whisker;

clean as a whistle; a new broom sweeps clean; hand to mouth existence; too many cooks spoil the broth; might is right; one for the road; pour salt in the wound; a faint heart never won fair lady; busy as a bee; all thumbs; still water runs deep; eat crow; take it on the chin; give lip service; talk is cheap; don't go off half-cocked; drunk as a skunk; quick as a weasel; pride goeth before a fall; independent as Job's off ox; prune face; here's mud in your eye; the college of hard knocks; it's tougher where there's none; homely as sin; off the hook; all's well that ends well; nothing ventured, nothing gained; every dog has its day; take a hike; stretch the truth; a fine kettle of fish; drag your feet; make both ends meet; proud as a peacock; man before beast; a lame excuse; get a move on; like shooting fish in a barrel; blow your top; knee high to a grasshopper; water over the dam; tickled pink; make your own bed; feather your nest; off the hook; lip service; bite the bullet; on tenterhooks; right off the bat; crooked as a string and as they all say: Quit while you're ahead.

Two Different Worlds

Over the holidays I observed my teenage grandchildren and some of their activities. The four young people are all involved with computers—games, the Internet and email. They have digital cameras, which I don't understand, and I guess they copy and share all kinds of things with telephones that take and send pictures.

I don't understand the technology and I think, in their eyes, the only thing that saves me from being a complete old fogy is that, at age eighty-eight, I still ride a motorcycle.

As a child, my world was not a color TV set. It was a simpler world that often meant creating my own amusements. They don't recall or miss pea shooters, wooden slingshots, scooters, kick the can, kazoos, Jew's harps, saving Indian head pennies, Tom Mix rings, milking a cow, driving a team of horses, hoeing the family garden, pulling weeds, picking off potato bugs, polishing and waxing a car, churning butter, pushing a lawnmower, homemade ice cream, picking apples, felling a tree, sawing wood, shoveling coal, hauling ashes out, riding an open-air trolley, digging worms, walking to school, a taffy pull and, least of all, painting a car with a brush.

My childhood left me with a bunch of warm memories that reflect more homespun times. But as is said: "No matter how much you would like it to be, you can't go back to the past."

MY SWAN SONG

It has always been my thinking that some people don't know when to quit. Look at the sports figures that, because of the money and notoriety, stayed long beyond their prime.

With no time limits for politicians, many old fools in Congress with their antiquated thinking continue to milk the public cow. I'm sure most of them went to Washington full of high ideals, and a fire in their bellies to do great things. As the years went by, the system and the perks hooked them. Many are still feathering their nests while ours fall apart.

In my limited sphere through the years, I have had the satisfaction of putting my nonsense down on paper and seeing it published by the Granby *Drummer*, *Southwoods* magazine, and *Stonewalls* magazine.

I have the feeling that I've written for too long because, at age eighty-seven, I've outlived the readers who can understand my reminiscences. If you're under sixty-five, you don't remember Pearl Harbor, Franklin Delano Roosevelt, WWII or Harry S. Truman.

I've had fun writing about my younger days on my grandfather's farm in North Granby during the 1930s. My stories are mostly BPH and BBP—before pantyhose and before ballpoint pens. After all, in my day most men wore soft felt fedora hats with a snap-brim and poetry rhymed.

What do people of this present day know about reading by a kerosene lamp, and the flickering shadows cast on the ceiling by a burning wick that shed light through a glass chimney.

In the days before Walmart, supermarkets and shopping on line, stores smelled like their particular line of business. I miss the recognizable aroma of an old-fashioned, wooden-floored hardware store, the nostalgia of a family bakery, a small fish market, single-counter diner, a shoeshine parlor, drug store, tobacco shop or repair garage. But then, I also miss the unmistakable aromas of horse stalls, chicken coops, cow barns, tobacco sheds, a silo, sawmills, a cider mill, bowling alley or a real feed store.

With my high school classmates of 1941, I lived the Big Band Era with the likes of Frank Sinatra, Bing Crosby and the girl singers who also traveled the circuit with bands like Tommy Dorsey and Harry James.

Traveling vaudeville acts were on the way out. The old theaters where they played were training ground for comedians like Bob Hope, Fred Allen, George Burns and Gracie Allen, Jack Benny and so many others.

I wrote about my stint in the Army Air Corps during WWII. In today's jet age, few remain who remember the sensations of real hands-on stick flying in a two-winged plane covered with painted canvass.

The mechanic stood by the propeller and when the pilot hollered, "contact," he lifted one knee high and gave a great downward pull on the wooden propeller. The engine fired to life and sputtered out a huge black cloud of exhaust. When it was warmed up and the chucks removed from in front of the wheels, the plane bumped along the uneven field to the smooth runway.

Sitting in that open cockpit with goggles on, hearing the roar of the full-throttled engine, feeling the air swirling all around you and looking down at familiar hillsides so far below, was breathtaking.

Some time later I was assigned to a B-17 Flying Fortress bomber. I can still feel the two-minute pitch, roll and yaw as we flew at altitude, and the roar of its four Wright Cyclone engines outfitted with Hamilton Standard propellers as it clawed at the upper air.

Even now I sense the great rush of air through the plane as the bomb bay doors opened. The pronounced lightening of the ship as the heavy bombs dropped over our targets. I still feel the cutting edge of the oxygen mask on my cheeks and smell the coolness of the oxygen.

When the war was finally over, I had to have a car. I was working as a clerk for $125 a month so I couldn't afford much. I bought a 1933 Ford Phaeton (a four-door convertible). It didn't look like much, so I bought some fine sandpaper and some black Ducco enamel paint. I sanded the whole car and then, using a three-inch-wide brush and overlapping strokes at right angles to each other, I painted it. There were some small brush marks, so I hand rubbed it using fine rubbing compound. When I was done, it looked great: I used rubberized white paint to top it off with white-walled tires.

I think back to the farm in the 1930s and the 1928 four-door Whippet. Do you recall hand cranking a car to get it started? How about fixing a flat by jacking up the car, taking the wheel off and removing the inner tube to glue a patch on it? Then pumping the tire up by hand and putting it back onto the car?

I'd be hard pressed to find a youth of today who could replace and gap a set of spark plugs, change and set the distributor points and use a timing light to make the engine run even. How about changing the oil and filter or relining the brakes? Perhaps I'll ask my young neighbor whether or not he knows how to hand milk a cow, drive a team of horses or reach under a nesting hen to gather her warm eggs for breakfast?

I don't think he would understand driving a mowing machine with a team of horses and using a one-horse, two-wheeled rake to make long windrows of hay. Could he use a pitchfork and roll those rows into haycocks? If he mastered that, could he pitch the hay onto the wagon and pitch it up to the hayloft?

Do any of you recall picking an apple crop in the fall? I still feel the pressure on the bottoms of my feet as I stood on the rungs of a tall ladder that narrowed at the top to reach the uppermost branches.

My arms remember the impact of the axe blade biting into a ten-inch tree trunk to knock it down for firewood. Small limbs were chopped off and the long poles dragged to the woodshed by the Belgian workhorses.

A water-cooled engine called a "one-lunger" or "make and break" powered the saw blade by means of a wide leather pulley belt. As the blade whirled, a pole was fed into it and cut to twelve-inch lengths. The lengths were split with an axe on the chopping block to fit into the kitchen stove.

In that same era, I enjoyed riding in the rumble seat of a 1930 Model A Ford and appreciated the purr of a well-tuned engine. I may look up at the stars now, but it doesn't compare with stargazing from that rumble seat with a pleasant date by my side.

As I near the close, how many are left who built their own kites and covered them with newspaper? Did you use old rags for a tail? Did you cut a small square of paper and send it up the kite string as a message?

As I finish this, I'm glad to use a ballpoint pen rather than the scratchy metal point I dipped into an inkwell to write on coarse school paper.

A dwindling number of people recall steam beds for tobacco seedlings. A few know about putting up cloth for shade grown tobacco. Some may have crawled on their hands and knees in intense summer heat dragging a canvass container to hold the maturing leaves you picked from the stalk. Maybe you used a thick needle and string to sew the leaves onto a lath, or climbed the rafters to hang the leaves to dry.

Gone are the days of ring-a-leavio; olly olly in free; hopscotch; jump rope; one-a-cap; pin the tail on the donkey; spin the bottle and post office. No more taffy pulls or dipping for apples. No more pulling petals from a daisy and saying, "she loves me; she loves me not." No more playing jacks or shooting marbles.

Yes, I'm sure it's true that "every dog has its day," and I've had mine. It's been a good run, and I appreciate the readers who have followed my ramblings. For them, these simple words will have to do—Thank You and Goodbye.

Lightning Source UK Ltd.
Milton Keynes UK
UKOW04n2243071217
314063UK00002B/75/P